MAR

VENICE

with Local Tips

The author's special recommendations are highlighted in yellow throughout this guide

There are five symbols to help you find your way around this guide:

★
Marco Polo's top recommendations – the best in each category

sites with a scenic view

places where the local people meet

places where young people get together

(96/A1)
pages and coordinates for the Street Atlas of Venice
(O) *area not covered by maps*

MARCO POLO

Travel guides and language guides in this series:

Alaska • Algarve • Amsterdam • Australia/Sydney • Bahamas • Barbados
Berlin • Brittany • California • Canada • Channel Islands • Costa
Brava/Barcelona • Costa del Sol/Granada • Côte d'Azur • Crete • Cuba
Cyprus • Dominican Republic • Eastern Canada • Eastern USA • Florence
Florida • Gran Canaria • Greek Islands/Aegean • Ibiza/Formentera • Ireland
Istanbul • Lanzarote • London • Mallorca • Malta • Mexico • New York
New Zealand • Normandy • Paris • Prague • Rhodes • Rome • San Francisco
Scotland • South Africa • Southwestern USA • Tenerife • Turkish Coast
Tuscany • USA: Southern States • Venice • Western Canada

French • German • Italian • Spanish

Marco Polo would be very interested to hear your comments and suggestions. Please write to:

North America:
Marco Polo North America
70 Bloor Street East
Oshawa, Ontario, Canada
(B) 905-436-2525

United Kingdom:
GeoCenter International Ltd
The Viables Centre
Harrow Way
Basingstoke, Hants RG22 4BJ

Cover photograph: Gondoliere (Bavaria)
Photos: H. Hartmann (32); K. Kallabis (14, 67); Mauritius: Ascher (40), Beck (11, 72), Bohnacker (70), Cupak (62), Ditges (27), Kolley (7), Ley (95), Messerschmidt (44), Photo Bank (31), Pigneter (21), Scholey (25), Waldkirch (74), Witzgall (33); D. Renckhoff (4, 18, 54, 61); Transglobe Agency: Allgöwer (34), Boyer (76), Krüger (50), Winsnes (82)

2nd revised edition 2000

Author: Rainer Stiller
Translator: Joan Clough
English edition 2000: Gaia Text
Editorial director: Ferdinand Ranft
Chief editor: Marion Zorn
Cartography for the Street Atlas: © Hallwag AG, Bern
Design and layout: Thienhaus/Wippermann
Printed in Germany

CONTENTS

REALE MUTUA
ASSICURAZIONI

Discover Venice!

The venerable city on the lagoon, touched by the chill hand of mortality, is more alluring than ever

Ghosts over her paving stones. Probably no other city in the world has been linked with death (in literature, painting and film) so often as Venice. Don't Look Now but if you do, you'll still be enchanted by what you see. It won't be frightening or even depressing. The feeling that the city is mortal is simply a fact of life in Venice just as the waxing and waning moon makes the waves lap against the city walls and subside at high and low water.

A person who, like Gustav von Aschenbach in Thomas Mann's 'Death in Venice', suffocates in the 'repellent mugginess' of the city, is bound to view Venice differently from someone who brings a healthy curiosity to it as well as eagerness to learn, fortified by lots of good advice and even some insider tips for getting the most out of a stay here. The German poet Rainer Maria Rilke was just such a traveller in 1910, willing to forget all prejudices for and against the city and simply bask in its magic: 'Beautifully counteracting this world, its very decoration charged with latent energies tingling through ever finer nerves: this Venice.' You reach it – no matter where you've come from or how you've arrived – only by water. Even travellers who arrive at Santa Lucia Central Station, humbly clutching suitcases for a stay of just one or two nights, can reach their hotels in the *centro storico*, the historic city centre, only by being packed into the next *traghetto* for their first ride in a gondola and crossing the Canal Grande. A more majestic way of arriving is, of course, to take a *vaporetto*, a water bus operated by the public transport lines, or even a *motoscafo*, a water taxi, with room for four – no more. When you touch down at Marco Polo Airport or come from the Lido at Iesolo, in clear weather, you'll see, as Goethe did from the mainland town of Fusina, Venice emerging like a pearl from the haze. Vittore Carpaccio, Giovanni Bellini, Giambattista Tiepolo – the names of those great painters we'll meet in the museums – come unbidden to mind the closer you draw to this unmistakable cityscape. 'Venice', as Peggy Guggenheim, patroness of the

The most stylish (but not cheapest) way of exploring the side canals is by gondola

arts, collector and unabashed hedonist whose art collection in the Palazzo Venier dei Leoni is a must on anyone's itinerary, repeated not long before she died in 1979, 'Venice – is art turned to stone.' The Venetians showed their appreciation by calling her 'the last of the Doges'.

The Doge was the visible sign of Venetian republican pride. As Niccolò Machiavelli reported in 1521: 'Venice grew out of the flight of people escaping to some islands at the head of the Adriatic Sea to avoid the perpetual wars which were always breaking out in Italy due to repeated barbarian incursions long after the fall of the Roman Empire. The island refugees began to live together without benefit of a prince to hand down decrees. They themselves enacted the laws which seemed to them best suited to their self-preservation. It worked out very well thanks to the long period of tranquillity which their geographical position ensured; for the sea barred access and those who devastated Italy had no ships to attack them.' The period described by Machiavelli was early, about 452 AD. From 697 the office of Doge existed, a title deriving from the Latin word for leader or duke 'dux'. Elected to office for life, the Doge was the head of state in the Republic of Venice and at first he ruled with absolute power. In 1032 an attempt to make the office of Doge hereditary failed, again due to stiff-necked Venetian republican pride. Indeed the aborted coup led to permanent limitation of the Doge's powers. The Venetian nobility continued to elect the Doge for life – while following a highly complex procedure – but six tribunes now watched over him, ensuring that he did not abuse his power. From 1310 the 'Dieci Inquisitori dello Stato', the Council of Ten, came into being, which was to become the republic's highest appellate court. In 1797 the office of Doge was abolished. Nowadays, the annual marriage festival, of the Doge to the sea, celebrated by the mayor of the city, recalls the historic office.

And, of course, the Doge's Palace is there, in the Piazza San Marco, a solid and enduring symbol of the power and glory of the Venetian Republic. Pigeons in their tens of thousands flutter in the square. San Marco is probably the best place for your first quick rendez-vous with the city. 'He whose heart does not beat faster when he is standing in the Piazza San Marco,' noted the Austrian writer Franz Grillparzer in the diary he kept in Italy, ' should have himself buried, for he is dead, irretrievably dead.'

Unfortunately, this is not entirely true in an era of mass tourism. Still, if you go to San Marco in the late afternoon, you may be lucky enough to find that the day-trippers who so often pack the square have left it to you. If you approach it from the mole, you'll see the powerful Palazzo Ducale, the Doge's Palace, on your right, with the Basilica San Marco behind it. On the left soars the Campanile, which you'll have to be patient to ascend (by lift) because long queues always form in front of

Above St Mark's Square towers the 100-m-high Campanile

it, even when it's raining. Next to the Campanile you enter the Piazza itself. It's surrounded by arcades and under them are two of the city's traditional meeting places: Caffè Florian on the left and Caffè Quadri on the right side. At the far end of the Piazza you go up to the Museo Civico Correr, which is renowned throughout the world for the superb rotating exhibitions it mounts. By the way, there's a post office on the narrow side of the Piazza, behind the Ala Napoleonica. San Marco is also the name of the section of the city round St Mark's Square. To be precise, Venice comprises six districts: Castello, Cannaregio, Santa Croce, San Polo, Dorsoduro (with La Giudecca) and, of course, San Marco. In addition, the municipality of Venice includes the mainland districts of Marghera and Mestre, four km distant across the water, as well as the Lido and the islands of Burano, Murano and Torcello. Built on 118 islands in all and linked by 177 canals and more than 400 bridges, Venice is the capital of the region of Veneto. Covering nearly 13.5 square km, Venice has a population of approximately 340,000 although more residents than ever are leaving to settle on the mainland. Here are some figures to illustrate how rapidly the historic city is becoming depopulated: in the past 30 years alone the population of the *centro storico* has declined by more than fifty per cent, decreasing from 176,000 to not more than

70,000 at present and the trend continues.

There are two reasons for the move to the mainland: tourism and ecological factors. Nearly 2.5 million visitors come to Venice a year and spend several days whereas nearly 10 million pop in annually just to say they've seen the pearl of the lagoon. Since most of these visitors don't stray beyond the historic centre, the main squares tend to be packed. Most Venetians prefer just to come over to work. This attitude, too, looks back on a long tradition in Venice. During the Middle Ages, la Serenissima, Her Serene Highness, as the citizens of Venice used to style their republic in a flight of modesty, was one of the known world's most flourishing, richest and powerful cities. Nowadays, affluence is not generated by trade and commerce. Venice is a hub of tourism and, as such, has strained its capacity for handling the volume of visitors to the utmost. Again figures suffice: 225 hotels with 14,000 beds and 1,700 private rooms.

The second reason so many Venetians choose not to reside in their city is an ecological one. Venice does not smell as much as it once did since wells for natural gas and drinking water may no longer be drilled. However, the environmental protection measures already enacted cannot reverse the damage done to Venice over the centuries. After the terrible flood of 1966 all sorts of plans for a tidal barrier and other projects to prevent regular flooding and, therefore, keep the city from sinking into the water have been mooted, but so far they have come to nothing. Venice continues to subside – and you'd be well advised to pack a pair of wellies for keeping your feet dry when you come here. Just a touch of wind and rain and the Piazza San Marco is under a sheet of water you'll have to clatter through on planks.

'Adesso basta!' Riccardo Held, a young poet, translator, homme de lettres and dyed-in-the-wool Venetian, refuses to listen to all those worst-case scenarios allegedly hanging over his native city: 'Enough is enough!' We're standing in a little bar in Dorsoduro. On a Sunday morning. Other men are standing with us in the bar – having a *ciacole*, an after-church chat. The Venetians are doing it in the melodious vernacular which bears as little resemblance to standard Italian as the Welsh lilt does to clipped Received Pronunciation.

The men are drinking *un bicchiere di bianco*, a little glass of white wine or perhaps two or even three before lunch. The subject of their conversation is football, or the most recent cycle race or even – since we're not far from the Accademia here – a book they're reading. 'Venice,' as Riccardo says, 'is not decline and fall. Venice stands for all forms of art.' And that, naturally, includes the art of living!

The bar empties just as quickly as it filled when the clanging of church bells died down. We put L1,500 or at most L2,000 – it's never more than that here – on the counter to pay for our wine and walk out. Riccardo, who like most of the others is going home for Sunday lunch, has suggested I head east through Dorsoduro to the tip of the island. On the way I'll find a tiny trattoria serving *gnocchi alla salvia,* succulent little potato dumplings scented with sage and smoothed with butter. Then I go on down the waterfront pavement known as the Záttere, past the berths of the boats that also cross to the island of La Giudecca. Even the Venetians disagree on what the name of this island off to the south means. It may derive from Jews, *giudei,* or convicts, *giudicati,* those judged and found guilty. At any rate, La Giudecca is an integral part of Venetian history, a place to which Venetians often had to retreat and did. The island had monasteries for voluntary residents, prisons for those forced to reside here and slums for the no-hopers. Venetians bear witness every year to the island's status as part of the city by staging a festival on it. On the third Sunday in July a pontoon bridge is run across from the Záttere pavement to La Giudecca and the feast of the Church of the Redeemer (Redentore), which Palladio was commissioned to build in observance of a vow after plague had devastated the city in 1576, is celebrated.

As you walk on, leaving the Church of the Redentore behind you, Chiesa Santa Maria della Salute looms into view at the tip of Dorsoduro. Piazza San Marco looks so close you could reach out and touch it. Even though you're soon overcome with a feeling that it's impossible not to lose your way in the labyrinth of alleys under the tiny bridges – Venice suddenly emerges here in all her gem-like clarity. The way back to the Ponte Accademia does not, however, simply follow the embankment of the Canal Grande. The alleys you take diverge from it but head you in the right direction, albeit disjointedly.

For timid visitors who manage to get lost even when they venture out armed with maps: yellow signs on walls point out the general direction – Accademia, Piazzale Roma, Rialto, San Marco. But watch out! Sometimes when you leave a narrow alley, all you'll find is a sign pointing back the way you thought you'd come. Or a bent arrow seems to direct you into a maze of at least three alleys which might be enough to faze even the most intrepid urban explorer. If you don't want to wander about aimlessly, ask a passer-by for directions. This may not always be the most reassuring course of action – especially after dark.

'In the glare of day, there is little poetry about Venice, but under the charitable moon her stained palaces are white again, their battered sculptures are hidden in shadows, and the old city seems crowned once more with the grandeur that was hers five hundred years ago. It is easy, then, in fancy, to people these silent canals with plumed gallants and fair ladies – with *Othellos and Desdemonas,* with *Iagos and Roderiogos* – with noble fleets and victorious legions returning from the wars. ... in the moonlight, her fourteen centuries of greatness fling their glories about her, and once more is she the princeliest among the nations of the earth.' Mark Twain, that knowing late 19th-century American abroad, hated to admit that he had succumbed to the spell of a place he describes so ambivalently in one of his classic accounts of his travels in the US and abroad, 'The Innocents Abroad'.

It can be cold here. And why shouldn't it be? After all, as Rilke put it, the city 'beautifully counteracts this world' and it does so at all times of the year, disclosing its secrets in spring, summer, autumn and winter, always to visitors' surprise and usually joy. There is in fact no ideal time for visiting Venice. It's always ideal.

All you have to do is look at the weather to find out when's the best time for you in Venice. May and the Indian summer of late September can spoil you with brilliant sunshine, burnishing the gold on innumerable St Mark's lions to its brightest. The summer months can be oppressively hot and muggy, especially when the water temperature at the Lido, at 24 °C (75 °F), is best for swimming. February often surprises visitors with clear, dry sunny days. October is the rainy season. November and January often find the city veiled in fog so thick that you literally have to squint to see your hand in front of your face. This also happens in December. Oddly enough, the crowds of tourists thin out to vanishing point at this time of year (and that's why so many hotels and restaurants are closed then). The spectral silence which settles on Venice at this time is a treat for connoisseurs. In his travel writings Horst Krüger reveals himself as that rare visitor who haunts the city in late December: 'Who would want to go to Venice three days before Christmas Eve? I've done just that again and again. What I found was a different Venice altogether, a supremely quiet Venice, just as it may have been in Goethe's day, as it must have been before tourism was invented. Venice without visitors: a strange experience. Certainly not for everyone. But for lovers of melancholy beauty and lovers of the extravagant something indeed. I speak for individualists, for eccentrics ... Venice in winter smells of coffee, red wine and dry firewood glowing to coals.'

Tranquility reigns until Epiphany, 6 January. Then the city prepares for a festival which – most Venetians seem to think so – has no significance any more: Carnival. By 14th January a scatter of masks has emerged from under the arcades of St Mark's Square. No one knows where they have come from nor where they are going. Only one thing is certain: they aren't from Venice. A few old Venetian families still give masquerade balls; however, they do so to entertain Italian guests and business acquaintances and friends from abroad. The traditional Venice Carnival was banished from the stage of history on 12 May 1797. When the last Doge was removed from office and the haughty 'Repubblica Serenissima' lost her independence to Austria – evidently Venetian society now had little to smile about behind those grinning masks. Carnival thrives today

Masqueraders fill the squares and alleys of Venice during the February Carnival season

thanks to the initiative taken by the Tourist Office in the 1970s. At that time concerns were voiced about Venice as a tourist attraction in foggy January and still chilly February. Arlecchino and Pantalone, Pulcinella and Colombina – the classic Commedia dell'arte masques improvised on stage are so much more delightful than the forced gaity of the turbulent goings-on in the streets – even though many a chalky-white painted face, above a form cloaked as early as noon flits across the squares masking only one intent and that the one expressed by the last real bard of the Venetian Carnival, Carlo Goldoni (1707–93), in the immortal words: 'Che dolce mestier di non far niente – what an agreeable profession doing nothing is!'

Wonder of wonders, the shops between St Mark's and the Rialto Bridge sell masks in all shapes and sizes – most of them hideous and not by any stretch of the imagination the work of craftsmen – all year round. You don't have to buy one!

Nonetheless, Venice, once queen of a mercantile empire, has remained an emporium. Lovely dresses, imaginative fabrics, hand-milled paper, leather goods, antiques – there's a lot to be discovered by the discerning shopper but not always at bargain prices. Shop around! The shop just round the corner may be selling its wares at a discount simply because its windows are not on the beaten tourist track (the same holds for restaurants, by the way).

Unlike most metropolises, Venice does not boast a single broad shopping thoroughfare worthy of the name. The *mercerie,* as shopping districts are called here, start – they're quite easy to find – in the shadow of the San Marco clock tower, just across the mole. Mazes of alleys criss-cross each other from here to the Rialto Bridge. Somewhere along the line they cease to be lined with shops and you find the shopping opportunities have simply petered out. The arcades of St Mark's house the most expensive and elegant shops in Venice. When you leave St Mark's Square across from the Campanile, you run into another long strip of small shops which extends to the Ponte Accademia and on beyond to the right towards the Piazzale Roma. This is where the best paper shops are as well as a sprinkling of antique shops, most of them specialist dealers in Art Nouveau and Art Déco.

The day you leave it's a good idea to shop for fresh pasta or some of that deliciously unusual bread to enjoy at home. Or you might visit one of the markets. One market that has retained its original charm is the fish market in the Campo della Pescheria near the Rialto Bridge. In Across the River and into the Trees, Hemingway has left an Expressionist sketch: 'In the market, spread on the slippery stone floor, or in their baskets, or their rope-handled boxes, were the heavy, gray-green lobsters with their magenta overtones that presaged their death in boiling water. ... There were many eels, alive and no longer confident in their eeldom. ... There were medium sized shrimp, gray and opalescent, awaiting their turn, too, for the boiling water and their immortality, to have their shucked carcasses float out easily on an ebb tide on the Grand Canal.'

Once back in the Piazza San Marco you might devote some thought to how you want to usher in the evening. A Campari bitter in the clock tower bar, which may not be as posh as the Florian or the Quadri under the arcades but is much livelier and more fun? It's a place where you stand and talk and pay at the till before your order comes – this is true of all bars in which you can have a quick *caffè* or a *panino,* a roll filled with all sorts of good things. Or a coffee in the lobby of the Danieli Hotel? This venerable hostelry of the rich on the Riva degli Schiavoni right on the Canale di San Marco is worth a visit just for a glimpse of its splendour, which, granted, has seen better days, but staying there is beyond most people's means. Or would you prefer to take your apéritif at the legendary Harry's Bar, most recently checked out by the FT, in the Calle Vallaresso, twenty paces from the Piazza? There you simply must try the fabulous Bellini, a cocktail consisting of puréed white peaches spiced according to a recipe which is a business secret and topped up with prosecco or, at your request, champagne. The first-floor restaurant (reservations must be made well in advance) has won numerous gastronomic awards. Although they aren't award-winners, there is a spate of small restaurants nearby serving tasty pasta and seafood at reasonable prices. All you have to do is keep your eyes open and follow your nose and you'll light on one of these in any narrow side alley.

After you've had such a satisfying evening meal, you'll find that Venice has a lot to offer for night owls. Toss off a heady nightcap and on to – their number has been growing recently – bars, pubs, student cafés with live music. If that doesn't seem like enough of a choice to you, bacaros are usually open till long past midnight and they are certainly long on atmosphere. A night on the town doesn't mean that you should make a big thing about rising early the next morning. Away from the historic core of the city there are so many things to see and do. The classic programme includes a visit to at least one of the islands dotted about the lagoon.

Burano (pop. approx 5,000), whose residents earn their livelihood by fishing and working in tourism, might be one to start with. They sell to tourists what they assure is 'hand-woven bobbin lace' underwear but most such wares come from the Far East nowadays. Making bobbin lace is a trade which has become obsolete here. However, the famous glass is still free-blown and hand-twisted on the neighbouring island of Murano but there, too, business with affluent and gullible visitors is booming. The bulk wares produced in Murano overflow into the shops round St Mark's and most of these objects are simply knick-nacks.

The most important island near Venice is still the Lido with its beaches and fine hotels. Luchino Visconti filmed Tomas Mann's novel 'Death in Venice' in one of them, the Grand Hôtel des Bains. Cinema as a medium and an industry plays an important role in Venice by any standards. Once a year the Film Festival is held in the big local cinema, the Excelsior Hotel and the Casino and attracts a galaxy of stars. The Venice Film Festival has taken place in late August and early September since 1932 and shares its reputation as the world's most important event of its kind with the Cannes Film Festival on the Côte d'Azur. 'The Film Festival', writes Erica Jong in chapter 12 of 'Fear of Fifty. A Midlife Memoir', 'was a madhouse ... an unexpected invitation came to me to be a judge in the Venice Film Festival. ... I immediately accepted. ... All day, the jury watch movie after movie – the best, the worst, the mediocre. ... The wonder of this festival and its spontaneous combustion got me thinking of my Venice novel [Serenissima] again. Every writer wants to go back in time as long as the future safely waits to be returned to. ... everyone got publicity – whether they wanted it or not. And the city of Venice got its money's worth from the celebrities it paid to fly and feed.'

That sounds hard – and is only part of a multi-faceted image. If Venice were as publicity-oriented and superficial as that, it would not have remained such a magnet for visitors down through the centuries. Nor would it have been historically of such great significance – and this despite the threat hanging over it – as it has been. The Film Festival is only a contemporary facet, unlike the little Jewish cemetery on the Lido, which was laid out in the 14th century, or the 11th-century church of San Nicolò near it.

On our way back from the Lido by *vaporetto* we suddenly remember why San Nicolò seemed so familiar. Our memories were jogged by the sight of a passing *motoscafo* belonging to a firm of undertakers although there was no coffin in it because funerals only take place in the mornings in Venice. We know San Nicolò from the Roeg film in which Donald Sutherland plays a church restorer and a red-robed, murderous dwarf lurks in the alleys: 'Don't Look Now'. When the fog closes in on you and the way back to your hotel seems long, the chill hand of mortality that menaces this beautiful but spectral city seems to touch your shoulder and you really are afraid to look behind you.

CONTINENTAL

Exploring the city

Venice looks like a maze till you're used to it – explore it bit by bit and on foot if possible

'A great deal has been told and printed about Venice', wrote the poet and privy councillor Johann Wolfgang von Goethe in 1786 in his travel diary 'so I do not want to be circumlocuitous in describing it. I shall relate how I encounter it. What I notice is, however, the populace, the mass of it, a necessary and arbitrary state of being.' As a modern visitor to Venice, you can learn something from those Venetians Goethe scorned. A clever statistician has calculated that Venetians spend two hours a day going through their city's alleys on foot. They know this is the best way of going from A to B here. It's nearly always more expeditious, once you know the way, to go on foot than to take a *vaporetto* from one landing-stage to another. After all, you do have to factor in the time spent going to and from the vaporetto's mooring.

Going on foot opens up unexpected opportunities for exploring. A glimpse into one of the many *corti*, one of the lovely courtyards of the Venetian Palazzi, or a brief venture into one of those culs de sac known as *rami*, branching off so many of the narrow streets and alleys here – pedestrians have right of way or at least a choice.

A trip on the Canal Grande shows you the most important sights

We shouldn't neglect to mention that exploring Venice from the water is, of course, as exciting as you've always thought it would be. You may like the comfortable swaying motion of the gondola which wafts you – they're not cheap – to the highlights of la Serenissima. Gondolieri know their way around – and won't take you the long way round because tour prices are calculated in units of 50, 75 oder 100 minutes.

Approaching Venice by water bus is the most entertaining trip of all and you'll see a lot this way. You'll probably be fortunate enough to be caught up in a crowd of friendly Venetians conversing in their lilting voices and attuning you to the city. This is the cheapest means of transportation for sightseeing here because a single ticket will take you pretty far.

The best lines for sightseeing by water bus are the no. 1 and no. 82 lines. The no. 1 line stops more frequently than the no. 82 and goes the full length of the

Canal Grande. Starting at the Piazzale Roma, it stops at every landing-stage along the Bacino di San Marco Basin before going across to the Lido. The no. 82 line in the opposite direction starts at the Rialto Bridge, with stops at San Marcuola, Ferrovia, Piazzale Roma and Tronchetto and continuing on through the Giudecca Canal to San Giorgio, San Zaccaria and San Marco and back again into the Canal Grande. This line also goes to the Lido after a further stop.

It's up to you when you'd like to be underway. Certainly St Mark's Square is particularly lovely in the early morning when the caffès are just beginning to crank up their window rollshutters – when it still looks sleepy – but you're feeling venturesome. Other may prefer to wait until noon, before the pigeons are sated from the ministrations of overly solicitous tourists, both flocking in their hundreds into St Mark's. Bustle and languor, showy splendour and hidden beauty, famously mysterious – Venice invites you!

BRIDGES

The real Venice landmarks are the *ponti*. Bridges are what link the numerous tiny and minuscule islands to form the pearl of the lagoon. There must be about 400 of them – no one has ever taken the trouble to count – crossing and recrossing the 177 canals. When they were used by

MARCO POLO SELECTION: SIGHTSEEING

1 Campanile
The bell tower, essential to Venetian well-being (page 33)

2 Chiesa Santi Giovanni e Paolo
The massive church where eleven Doges are buried (page 29)

3 Ghetto
A quarter be off the beaten track that deserves better (page 32)

4 Giardini Pubblici
A patch of green in this city of water and stone (page 31)

5 Goldoni Monument
It marks the liveliest spot in the city (page 22)

6 Marco Polo House
Need we really explain why? (page 24)

7 Piazza San Marco
If not this one, which square in Venice? (page 32)

8 Palazzo Vendramin-Calergi
A gem, once Wagner's residence, now a winter casino (page 19)

9 Ponte di Rialto
Orientation for everything in Venice (page 17)

10 Torcello
For rest and relaxation, take a break (page 26)

equestrian cavaliers and by peasants' yokes of oxen, the bridges were very low, nearly on pavement level and made of wood. Not until these low wooden affairs seriously hindered boat traffic were they replaced by arched stone bridges. Gondolieri can pass under them standing up to propel their gondolas. Now pedestrians are at a disadvantage because they will have to clamber up and down so many times during a day spent on foot. Some Venetian bridges have become world-famous.

Ponte dell'Accademia (101/E4)
This has been a temporary bridge since long before WWII. During the 1930s the city authorities were undecided about how the San Marco and Dorsoduro districts should be linked here. Since the mid-19th century there had been a bridge in the same place, built according to plans by the Austrian A.E. Neville, but the city council even discussed tunnelling under the Canal Grande where the bridge is. Even today local politicians tend to refer to the subject when they can't think of anything else to contribute to council sessions. The Accademia Tunnel project has, therefore, not been entirely written off. A practical tip: when it rains the wooden treads of this bridge are treacherously slippery, which can be dangerous, especially when you're descending the bridge. *Mooring: Accademia*

Ponte delle Guglie (96/C2)
This bridge is easy to recognize by the four distinctive tapering obelisks with which it ends. It spans the Canale di Cannareggio, the second widest canal in Venice after the Canal Grande, linking the section near the train station and the Campo San Geremia with what was once the Jewish ghetto. Built in 1580, the bridge is broad and single-arched. At its foot is a little fish and vegetable market, which is popular with Venetians. *Mooring stop: Guglie*

Ponte della Paglia (103/D3)
Sometimes so beset with photographers that you can scarcely see it, this bridge affords the best view of another, much more famous one: The Bridge of Sighs. The Ponte della Paglia links the San Marco Molo (mole) with the Riva degli Schiavoni, where the Dalmatians, called Slaws *(schiavoni)* by the Venetians, used to moor their fishing boats and sell their fresh catches. On one of the piers you'll see the relief of the 'Madonna of the Gondolieri,' dating from the 16th century. *Mooring: San Zaccaria*

Ponte di Rialto (98/B5–6)
★ The Rialto Bridge links the San Marco and San Polo districts. It is a traffic hub geared to tourists, as you can easily see from the dreadful souvenirs sold on the bridge. By the 11th century Rialto was a major commercial centre – the vegetable and fish market recall its heyday. In fact it was once of Europe's most important trade centres. The Venetian ducat enjoyed the same status in those days as the German Mark does in the late 20th century. At that time there was a pontoon bridge across the Canal Grande. In 1264 it was

replaced by a wooden bridge, which was demolished during a popular revolt in 1310. Although it was rebuilt, it didn't last long because it broke down under the weight of the procession attending the nuptials of the Marchioness of Ferrara. An attempt to span the Canal Grande with a drawbridge which would enable large boats to pass through failed. A new bridge was necessary and was finally built between 1588 and 1592. Antonio Da Ponte was the architect who designed the 48-m-long and 22-m-wide bridge you see today. It rests on 12,000 piles driven into the bed of the canal. It was built of stone to last – good piece of Venetian engineering. *Mooring stop: Rialto*

Ponte degli Scalzi (96/B3)
A stone structure built at the same time as the Ponte dell' Accademia Bridge, the Ponte degli Scalzi links the railway station with the San Polo section. It marks the shortest route to the centre of Venice. *Mooring: Ferrovia*

Ponte dei Sospiri (103/D3)
Yes, and then there's the Bridge of Sighs. The most frequently photographed, the subject of poems, it links the Doge's Palace with what was once the prisons, the notorious lead chambers where Giacomo Casanova was incarcerated. Fortunately for him, the great lover was able to flee this terrible prison, which gave the bridge its name. After

The no. 1 water-bus line putters down the length of the 'Canalazzo' and then crosses to the Lido: the ideal sightseeing tour for newcomers to Venice

receiving their sentences, the condemned passed, weeping over it, to their cells. *Mooring: San Zaccaria*

Ponte delle Tette **(97/F5)**
This bridge will put you in a more cheerful mood. In the 16th century, San Polo was a place Casanova would have liked. Girls bared their breasts in open windows round the Bridge of Tits – with the blessing of the authorities. The story goes that this was the officially sanctioned method of sex education for straights when homosexuality was rife in Venice. *Mooring: San Silvestro*

CANAL GRANDE

Venice's 'High Street', the Canal Grande or 'Canalazzo', as the Venetians call it, winds sinuously through the city in the form of an inverted S past palaces, churches and houses. This is just the place for discussing some of the buildings it passes. Like so many travellers, we'll begin our trip on the Canal Grande, where you can take a water bus – we recommend the slower no. 1 line with all those stops along the way – or by private gondola, a much more expensive undertaking, at Santa Lucia Station. This is a building which assumed its present appearance in the mid-1950s. We'll describe the buildings as we pass them on the Canal and so their names will not – for a welcome change – be in alphabetical order.

Chiesa degli Scalzi **(96/B3)**
This church – officially known as Santa Maria di Nazareth – is near the station on our left at the foot of the bridge of the same name at the centre of the city. The Carmelite Order commissioned Baldassare Longhena to build it between 1670 and 1680. He also built the church of Santa Maria della Salute, at the end of our trip on the Canal. *Landing-stage: Ferrovia*

Palazzo Labia **(96/C2)**
The palace on the left-hand side of the Canal today houses the Venice branch offices of RAI, the state radio and television conglomerate. The building is impressive and even more so the frescoes in the first-floor festival hall. They were executed by Giambattista Tiepolo in 1757. *Landing-stage: Guglie*

Palazzo Vendramin-Calergi **(97/E2–3)**
★ Again on the left-hand side is an early 16th-century building which exemplifies the Lombard style of that period. From summer 1882 Richard Wagner lived here briefly with his family and servants. The German composer died here on 13 February the following year. This palazzo is well worth a visit even by those who don't intend to go into the casino which it houses during the winter months. *Landing-stage: San Marcuola*

Ca' d'Oro **(98/A4)**
Even people who are not culture vultures, loathe museums and give the Galleria Franchetti a miss should cast a glance at this palace, like the above to our left. Generally regarded as the most magnificent example of Venetian High Gothic secular architecture extant, it has been me-

ticulously restored in years of painstaking, scholarly work. The only thing about it that has not be restored is the gold which originally gave the building its name. The delicately articulated façade more than makes up for its absence. *Landing-stage: Ca' d'Oro*

Fabbriche Vecchie e Nuove (98/B5)

The upper floors of the two strikingly elongated rectangular structures on your right once housed the trade and commerce authorities of the Venetian Republic. Brisk trade was conducted under the arcades and still is. *Landing-stage: Rialto*

Fondaco dei Tedeschi (98/B5)

Rebuilt in 1508 after a fire in 1505, the house before the Rialto Bridge on your left was a hostelry for 'Germans' *(tedeschi):* Austrian and South German merchants and bankers. The Augsburg banking house of Fugger retained rooms here and luminaries of Renaissance art such as Albrecht Dürer used the Fondaco as their Venice headquarters. Titian and Giorgione decorated the façade with frescoes. A fragment has been preserved in the Ca' d'Oro. The Fondaco houses the main post office. *Landing-stage: Rialto*

Palazzo dei Camerlenghi (98/B5)

Built between 1525 and 1528, the fine Renaissance building diagonally across from the Fondaco was of major importance to the Republic of Venice with its far-flung mercantile outposts as its Finance Court. Venetian merchants were implacable in dealing with debtors and sentences pronounced by the Court were harsh. The debtors' prison was located conveniently on the ground floor of the building. *Landing-stage: Rialto*

Riva del Vin (98/A–B6)

Wine casks were once unloaded at the quai on the far side of the Rialto Bridge. Souvenir shops and restaurants have since mushroomed here. *Landing-stage: Rialto*

Palazzo Giustinian (101/D2)

A broad façade conceals two buildings separated by a narrow passage. In 1858/59 Richard

Five years' delivery period

The gondola is the emblem of Venice. They are very sophisticated boats, made of wood and weighing 400 to 500 kg. For centuries they have been standardized with a uniform length of 10.15 m. The port side, where the gondolier stands is 24 cm longer so that the vessel can be rowed in a straight line. Since everything about a gondola is hand-made and there are ever fewer gondola makers, if you want one yourself, you'll have to wait at least five years for your order to be filled. Thomas Mann said of the standard gondola that it was 'a peculiar vehicle, handed down unaltered from the days of romantic ballads and so peculiarly black'. It costs L20,000,000.

Santa Maria della Salute has been erected on more than one million wooden piles

Wagner composed the second act of the opera 'Tristan and Isolde' in the right-hand palace. *Landing-stage: Ca' Rezzonico*

Palazzo Grassi **(101/D3)**
The Degli Antoni Baths were once housed in the 18th-century building diagonally across from it is now owned by the Fiat Foundation, which sponsors exhibitions acclaimed worldwide like the 1999 exhibition on Venetian and South German Renaissance art. *Daily 10 am–7 pm, admission L13,000, Landing-stage: San Samuele*

Santa Maria della Salute **(102/A-B5)**
On 21 November every year, a procession on the water to this church erected on more than one million wooden piles commemorates a vow made during a Plague epidemic. At the tip of

Dorsoduro, right on the Canal Grande. Worth a trip just to see Tintoretto's 'Marriage at Cana' and linger over it. *Daily 8.30 am–noon and 3 pm–6 pm, landing-stage: Salute*

MONUMENTS

In a city so rich in sights to see there are few monuments. The Venetian sense of dignity may have regarded personal monuments as crude. However, the Doges, counts, princes of the Church, merchants and bankers, including those at the Fondaco dei Tedeschi, did not object to being immortalized in the work of the greatest painters, a tradition begun in the Renaissance.

Colleoni Monument (99/D–E5)
Art historians tend to regard the equestrian statue of Bartolomeo Colleoni by the Florentine sculptor Andrea del Verrocchio as a supreme achievement of its kind. It commemorates the Condottiere Bartolomeo Colleoni, a swash-buckling figure in 15th-century Venice. In the service of the Republic he fought successful battles against Milan but more than once turned mercenary against the city on the lagoon. The monument was his own doing. On his death in 1475 he bequeathed an enormous legacy to Venice. Under the terms of his will, the city was only entitled to it if it commemorated the benefactor with a monument in front of the Basilica di San Marco. Confronted with such vulgar ostentation, the Senate was at a loss since even the Doges were not honoured with monuments there but arrived eventually at the following solution. Colleoni's will did not specify which San Marco was meant so they had the monument erected in front of the Scuola di San Marco next to the church of Santi Giovanni e Paolo. *Landing-stage: Ospedale*

Gobbo di Rialto (98/B5)
The name means the Hunchback of the Rialto. Across from the church of San Giacomo, he props up a ladder which in turn leads up to a short Egyptian marble column. All sorts of notices and ordinances, sentences, broadsheets and satirical writings have been posted on this 16th-century figure. Moreover, the Hunchback was notorious in the Middle Ages because he marked the end of the gauntlet run by convicted thieves, who were stripped naked and compelled to dash from St Mark's Square through the centre of the city, lashed by whips all the way to the Gobbo di Rialto. *Landing-stage: Rialto*

Goldoni Monument (98/B–C6)
★ Carlo Goldoni is one of only a select handful of playwrights who have really succeeded in making audiences split their sides laughing over the weaknesses thus exposed in human nature. Born in Venice in 1707, Goldoni studied law and did not devote himself to the theatre until the age of 40. His work represents the consistent development of commedia dell'arte in written form. In his comedies of manners, Goldoni literally tore the masks off his actors' faces. Plays like 'I rusteghi' (The Tyrants)' in Venetian dialect or 'La

Locandiera (The Mistress of the Inn)', the latter once a vehicle for the Duse, are still performed. In a quirky touch of empathy, the bronze Goldoni smirks quizzically in the lively Campo San Bartolomeo. *Landing-stage: Rialto*

CEMETERIES

Churches were only permitted by law to bury the dead in graveyards behind them until the mid-19th century. The office of conveying and burying the dead was still performed by *becchini*, grave-diggers, who pursued their grim trade in ornately carved gondolas shrouded in black. In compliance with sanitary regulations exacted by the Venetian Senate, the dead were then ferried to the soft swish of long oars to the island of San Michele off the long waterfront called the Fondamenta Nuova. Today noisy *motoscafi* serve as hearses. The grave-diggers – no longer called *becchini,* but *sterratori* instead, which means earthworkers – carry coffins from the landing stage into the church and to the grave, which often entails a 15-minute walk.

Cimitero Comunale San Michele (O)

The municipal cemetery on San Michele is breaking out of its walls. Because the subsoil at San Michele is waterlogged, Venetians prefer to bury their dead in the honeycomb of wall niches *(oculi),* in the vernacular disrespectfully dubbed *fornetti* (little ovens). As a result, the cemetery walls are cracking. There is little money for restoration although in 1998 David Chipperfield, an English architect, won a competition for enlarging and redesigning the cemetery. As it is now, sections of it are depressing. A friendly attendant helps visitors to seek out the graves of famous people buried here. Sergei Diaghilev (1929), impresario of the Paris Ballets russes, is buried in the Orthodox section, as is his colleague, the composer Igor Stravinsky (since 1971), and, in the Protestant section, the American poet and Fascist sympathiser Ezra Pound (since 1972). *Landing-stage: Cimitero*

Cimitero Israelitico (O)

The modest Jewish cemetery is on the Lido not far from the church of San Nicolò. *Landing-stage: Lido*

HOUSES

In a city as rich as this one was for centuries, it is not surprising that magnificent palaces – private dwellings as well as public buildings – have been preserved. Some buildings and grounds fit into neither category yet are worth mentioning.

Giardini Pubblici (105/E–F6)

Even when the Biennale is not on, the Giardini Pubblici in the Castello district is a rewarding place to visit. The architecture of the various pavilions was adventurously avant-garde when they were designed and thus noteworthy in a city which otherwise tends to be conservative. Joseph Hoffmann (1870–1956), one of the founders of the Wiener Werkstätten, designed the *Austrian Pavilion* (built in 1933). The Dutch designer Ger-

The Barber of San Marco

Perhaps another Venice first: a barber who is a published poet. Angelo Guarraia has a tiny hairdresser's shop with one chair in the *Calle dei Stagneri o de la Fava no. 5233* (**98/C6**) in the San Marco district. However, in the back room he has a desk where he writes poetry. He has already published several volumes. Maybe he'll recite some of his work while he's cutting your hair *(8.30 am–12.30 and 3.30 pm–7.30 pm)*. You can't book in advance. Like most other haircutters, Angelo Guarraia's shop is closed on Mondays.

rit Thomas Rietveld (1888–1964) created the *Netherlands Pavilion* in 1954. Other noteable pavilions in these grounds are the *Venezuelan Pavilion* (also dating from 1954) by Carlo Scarpa (1906–78) and the *Finnish Pavilion* built in 1956 and designed by the celebrated Finnish architect Alvar Aalto (1898–1976). *Landing-stage: Giardini*

The Marco Polo House (98/C5)

★ The house in which the great traveller Marco Polo is said to have been born is in a tiny courtyard, the Corte del Milion, which is easy to miss if you're not looking out for it. The number of this house in the Cannaregio district is 5858 (entrance next to the church of San Giovanni Crisostomo). Polo, the famous son of a Venetian merchant, travelled through the Far East in the 13th century for 20 years. The account he penned of his travels, 'Il Milione', is still regarded by scholars as a reliable source of information. *Landing-stage: Rialto*

Mulino Stucky (100/A6)

Once it stood for advanced technology. Now Venice is no longer sure of what to do about this Neo-Gothic brick structure dating from 1882 on the island of La Giudecca. Discussion has gone on for years – with, as yet, no results to show for it – about converting the Stucky Mill into a cultural centre. *Landing-stage: Sant'Eufemia*

The Tintoretto House (98/A1)

The great painter Jacopo Tintoretto lived in this unpretentious house and died here on 31 May 1594. His pictures are scattered about Italy and the world – some are in the nearby church of the Madonna dell'Orto. *Fondamenta dei Mori, 3399, landing-stage: Orto*

ISLANDS

Burano (O)

The men fished and the women made bobbin lace. This was true of Burano a 100 years ago and to some extent still is. However, a strong dose of mass tourism has invaded the charming island (pop. nearly 6,000) – mainly because of its houses painted in lovely Venetian colours. It once also sustained a sizeable artists' colony, presumably for the same reason. A permanent *exhibition* in the Consorzio Merletti is exhaustive on the art of

Burano and the other lagoon islands are quieter than Venice

making bobbin lace. The trip by boat from Venice takes three-quarters of an hour. *Exhibition Wed–Mon 10 am–5 pm, admission L8,000, landing-stage: Burano*

Murano (O)
On the glass-blowers' island there is a permanent exhibition in the Vetrario on this exacting craft (see the chapter on museums). *Landing-stage: Museo*

San Francesco del Deserto (O)
This magical island in the lagoon, where St Francis of Assisi once rested on his return from the Holy Land, is accessible only from Burano by water-taxi or private boat. Lending the island a Symbolist touch, the cypress-wreathed *monastery* hospitably opens its doors to the public Tues–Sun from 9 am to 11 am and 3 pm to 5 pm. There is no admission charge but the monks would be grateful for a small donation towards upkeep.

San Lazzaro degli Armeni (O)
Plague victims were tended here during medieval epidemics. Now the island is the spiritual and religious centre for Armenian Christians scattered across the world. Twelve monks cultivate Armenian religion and cultural traditions in a *monastery* founded in 1717. They show their collection of over 4,500 old manuscripts and books to visitors interested in incunabula. A

bookish but adventurous early 19th-century visitor, Lord Byron, found this island across from the bustling Lido delightfully restful. *Guided tours daily at 3.20 pm, admission L10,000, landing-stage: San Lazzaro*

Torcello **(O)**

★ This island is worth the trip because this was where Venice began. The other islands in the lagoon were settled from here. An absolute must for lovers of Veneto-Byzantine architecture: the *cathedral of Santa Maria dell' Assunta (daily 10.30 am–5.30 pm, admission L5,000).* Founded in 639, it is the earliest building (most of it dating from 1008) extant on the lagoon. Be sure to notice the beautifully coloured mosaic floor. There's a profane, albeit for gourmets equally urgent, reason for puttering out to Torcello: the trattoria. *Al Ponte del Diavolo. Landing-stage: Torcello*

CHURCHES

It would mean taking pigeons to St Mark's Square (instead of carrying coals to Newcastle) to imagine adding any more churches to those already in Venice. Church associations maintain there are 120 of them here and there is no point in even attempting to do justice to all of them. Some of them are small and overlooked by the hordes of tourists who flock to the lagoon. Great Venetian painters have worked in so many of their city's churches that you shouldn't be surprised to spot a superb Bellini, Titian or Tintoretto hung in a side-aisle and taken for granted. Venetian churches are open at very different times, a circumstance that makes planning to visit them pretty difficult. It goes without saying that, if you're not there to worship, you shouldn't burst into a church to sightsee during divine service. Please be suitably dressed when you do go into a church to look at it. At least 13 of the most beautiful Venetian churches charge for admission, including the Frari, the Redentore and St Mark's basilica. You can visit 6 churches with a ticket for L15,000 and tickets for one church cost L3,000. The revenue goes towards the upkeep of sacred buildings.

Basilica di San Marco **(103/D2)**

The aesthetic reservations Mark Twain had about St Mark's make refreshing reading after the culture vultures have had their say: 'Propped on its long row of low thick-legged columns, its back knobbed with domes, it seemed like a vast warty bug taking a meditative walk,' wrote Twain in A Tramp Abroad.

Bug or not, it has 2,463 legs though Twain only counted 500 interior columns while remarking (in The Innocents Abroad) that all those columns of porphyry, granite and marble were spoils brought by the Venetians from abroad. Now for some more 'masterfully ugly details', as Twain put it while conceding that the overall impression was one of harmony. More than 4,000 square metres of *mosaics*, the earliest dating from the 11th century, constitute the world's second largest (after Monreale in Sicily) mosaic surface. They have earned St Mark's the accolade of 'Basilica d'Oro' (the Golden Basilica). The *Pala d'Oro*, or altarpiece, glittered with gem-encrusted exuberance unmatched even in Istanbul before Napoleon's men looted it. Still richly set with gems, it once boasted 1,300 pearls, 400 garnets, 90 amethysts, 300 sapphires, 300 emeralds, 100 rubies, four topazes, not to mention all the gold and silver. The quadriga of gilt-bronze *Roman horses*, recently returned from a world tour to face St Mark's Square from an observation platform. This is the only ancient bronze quadriga extant. *Church: daily 9 am–6 pm, admission free; Pala d'Oro and cathedral treasure: Mon–Sat 9.30 am–4.30 pm, Sun 2 pm–4.30 pm, admission L3,000 and L4,000; galleries (with the four horses): daily 9.30 am–4.30 pm, admission L3,000; landing-stage: San Marco*

The 'Tetrarchs': famed sculpture on the Tesoro di San Marco

Carmini **(100/B3)**
Behind the second altar on the right in the 97-m-long centre aisle and across from a Lorenzo Lotto hangs a Cima da Conegliano, a lovely 'Adoration of the Shepherds', a Nativity (1509) set in the hilly Veneto landscape. *Campo Carmini, landing-stage: Ca' Rezzonico*

Gesuati **(101/D5–6)**
Don't be fooled by the Baroque façade. Inside hang Rococo paintings by Giambattista Tiepolo and Giovanni Battista Piaz-

Gondolieri aren't the only singers

In keeping with the worldwide trend towards proudly worn ethnicity, Venetians are rediscovering the beauties of their native dialect. It is quite different from standard Italian. Words have more richly subtle connotations and, what's more, the Venetian dialect sounds different from Italian, with its melodic lilt and soft consonants. Even if your Italian is limited to just a few phrases, try to strike up a conversation with a Venetian. Perhaps over an *ombra* – a word not used elsewhere in Italy for a little glass of wine before a meal. Typically Venetian, *Ombra* means obscuring (but not obfuscating) the real meaning of things, a shadow.

zetta. *Zàttere ai Gesuati, landing-stage: Zàttere*

Madonna dell'Orto **(O)**
Since Jacopo Tintoretto (1518–94) lived in this neighbourhood, it's only natural that this church and the Scuola Grande di San Rocco should give a sweeping survey of the painter's work. Ten large-scale works by the elder Tintoretto adorn the walls here, among them a startling and sombre 'Last Judgement'. Tintoretto and his children are buried in the apse of the church. *Fondamenta Madonna dell'Orto, landing-stage: Orto*

Pietà **(103/F2–3)**
Below this handsome ceiling fresco representing the 'Coronation of the Virgin' by Giambattista Tiepolo (1755), orphaned girls were taught choral and instrumental music by il prete rosso – none other than Antonio Vivaldi, before the building was used only as a church. *Riva degli Schiavoni, landing-stage: San Zaccaria*

Redentore **(O)**
In observation of a vow made during a plague epidemic in 1577, the Senate commissioned the renowned architect Andrea Palladio to design this church on La Giudecca. An annual procession comes to the church each year. *Campo Redentore, landing-stage: Redentore*

San Giorgio dei Greci **(103/F2)**
Orthodox divine service is celebrated every Sunday at 11 am in this, the oldest and most beautiful Greek Orthodox church outside the Greek culture area. It conceals a treasure of Byzantine and later *icons* in the Byzantine manner, an impressive addition to the collection housed in the neighbouring Icon Museum. *Salita dei Greci, landing-stage: Arsenale*

San Giorgio Maggiore **(103/E6)**
As early as the 10th century there was a Benedictine monastery on this island, once called the isle of cypresses; it's still well worth a visit because the monastery church was designed by the great Andrea Palladio after the mid-16th century. *Landing-stage: San Giorgio*

San Giovanni Crisostomo **(98/C5)**
Stone flowers and lions' heads outside and two superb altarpieces by Giovanni Bellini and Sebastiano del Piombo in this late 15th-early 16th-century church. *Campo San Giovanni Crisostomo, landing-stage: Rialto*

San Nicolò al Lido **(O)**
Parts of an 11th-century mosaic floor have been preserved in San Nicolò. The Doges attended high mass after the annual ceremony of the Marriage of Venice to the Sea. *San Nicolò, landing-stage: Lido*

San Salvatore **(102/B1)**
A superb painting makes this church a must for art lovers: a late Titian 'Annunciation'. *Campo San Salvatore, landing-stage: Rialto*

San Sebastiano **(100/A4)**
This was the church of the painter Paolo Veronese. His 'Coronation of the Virgin' hangs in the sacristy. The Veronese ceiling painting in the main aisle

Each house has a number

Pity the poor postman in Venice. The maze of alleys is confusing enough. The system of numbering houses is even worse! There is apparently no recognizable system behind the numbering. All that can be said is that each house in a district has a number instead of the usual street numbers. There are almost as many words for street as there are in English, including a plethora of diminutives to add to the medley: calle, calletta, callesella, calle larga, strada, lista, ruga, rughetta, salizzada, rio terrà, ramo, sottoportego, fondamenta, riva ... Any more questions about directions?

depicts the story of Esther. The two frescoes in the nuns' gallery recount the story of St Sebastian. Finally, the artist (d. 1588) is buried to the left of the main chapel. *Fondamenta San Basilio, landing-stage: San Basilio*

Santa Maria Gloriosa dei Frari (97/D6)
On entering the 'Frari', you'll spot Titian's funerary monument on your right. When the aged painter died of plague in 1576, the monks *frari* – Franciscans – simply ignored the Senate decree forbidding the burial of plague victims in churches. This church is almost a Titian museum in its own right, a circumstance which more than justifies the admission charge of L2,000. *Mon–Sat 9 am–6 pm, Sun 1 pm–6 pm (admission L3,000), Campo dei Frari, landing-stage: San Tomà*

Santa Maria dei Miracoli (99/D5)
Couples from Italy and abroad like to be married in this prime example of a Renaissance church. If you'd like to be married here, all you have to do is write to *Sposarsi a Venezia (Casella Postale 18, Venezia)* and ask for the forms. They will be sent to you with all the regulations pertain. *Campo Miracoli, landing-stage: Rialto*

Santi Giovanni e Paolo (99/E5)
★ When you consider how ornate the appointments and furnishings of so many Venetian churches are, this one looks restfully simple and austere but awesomely grand all the same. The nave was built to hold a large congregation so if you come here early in the morning, you'll feel rather lost all by yourself in this vast space. The Venetian dialect, which loves abbreviations and plays on words, has shortened this one, in which eleven Doges are buried, to 'San Zanipolo'. Right behind it are the grounds of the Venice General Hospital. *Campo Santi Giovanni e Paolo, landing-stage: Ospedale*

THE LIDO

(O) The main Venice beach is invariably packed in summer. The Lido is 12 km long and known for luxury hotels, gambling casinos and as the venue of the Venice Film Festival. *Boat routes from the train station and Piazzale Roma 1, 51, 52, 82; from the Riva degli Schiavoni as well as 6, 14; in* *summer the following additional water-bus lines: 61 and 62*

PALACES

It would be impossible to survey all the palaces belonging to the nobility and public buildings worthy of the name. The Venetians themselves have never counted them. Some have been described in the section on the Canal Grande. Here you'll be introduced to two more not mentioned elsewhere or if they are, are only briefly touched on. Notable all the same, this selection also includes – naturally *the* ultimate in Venetian palazzi, the Doge's Palace.

Palazzo Cappello (97/F5)
This building is haunted by the ghosts of two star-crossed lovers, a true Romeo and Juliet love story with some lurid twists. In the 16th century, fifteen-year-old Bianca Cappello was kidnapped by a banker and taken to Florence. He married her but was murdered. Then Bianca became the mistress of Francesco de Medici. In 1587 the lovers were poisoned. *Calle Bianca Cappello, landing-stage: San Silvestro*

Palazzo Contarini del Bovolo (102/A2)
The frequently photographed snail-like convolutions of this winding stair in a round courtyard tower have given this palazzo its name. The word for snail in Venetian dialect is *bovolo. Daily 10 am–6 pm, in winter 10 am–4 pm, admission L3,000, Calletta Contarini del Bovolo (approach from Campo Manin), landing-stage: Rialto*

Palazzo Ducale (103/D3)
The palazzo of palazzi! The residence of the Doges! The symbol of past Venetian power and glory! The west and south façades of the Doge's Palace measure 75 m and 71.5 m respectively. You enter the inner court through the Gothic *Porta della Carta,* with the flying stair known as the *Scala dei Giganti,* on which Doges-elect were seated at their inauguration ceremonies. The building is a museum from top to bottom. The rooms contain work by all the great Venetian painters. Particularly notable is the ceiling frieze in the Hall of the Great Council with 76 portraits of Doges by Jacopo Tintoretto and his son Domenico. Only one Doge is missing for the period between the 7th and 16th centuries. His portrait was obviously blacked out. The Latin inscription reads: 'This is the place of Marin Faliero, decapitated because he committed a crime.' In 1354 Faliero had tried to usurp sole power over Venice and was condemned to death. The portrait was blackened to warn all subsequent Doges that they were not to regard the Republic as their own property. *Daily 9 am–7 pm, winter 9 am–5 pm, admission L17,000 (incl. Museo Correr and other city museums), Piazzetta San Marco, landing-stage: San Marco*

PARKS

For obvious reasons Venice is not blessed with greenery. Only a very few hotels do at least have green courtyards. If you really feel better in a green space, you'll find only the following three possibilities.

The Doge's Palace represents the power and glory of the Republic of Venice

Giardini Pubblici (105/E–F6)
★ In the city park, the venue of the Venice Biennale art exhibition, there are some attractive paths with lots of benches to rest on and a bust of the composer Richard Wagner, who died in Venice. *Via Giuseppe Garibaldi, landing-stage: Giardini*

Giardino Papadopoli (96/A5)
This tiny park on the Canal Grande across from the Piazzale Roma is unfortunately very noisy. *Fondamenta Papadopoli, landing-stage: Piazzale Roma*

Parco delle Rimembranze (O)
Probably the best place of the three mentioned here for lovers of green spaces to rest and relax away from the Venetian hustle and bustle, this park is on the island of Sant'Elena off the Castello. *Viale Vittorio Veneto, landing-stage: Sant'Elena*

SQUARES

The *campi* are yet another characteristically Venetian feature. After losing your way in a maze of alleys and streets, you'll invariably come out into an open square, often with a church. The *campi* are still important venues for Venetians as gossip malls, children's playgrounds, football pitches and, not least, represent the perfect spot for all those Venetian cats to snooze in the sun. In Venice people arrange to meet – as they do on piazzas in the rest of Italy – on Campo So-and-So.

Campo San Bartolomeo (98/B–C6)
As already mentioned, this square with the bronze Goldoni Monument is the city's liveliest. *Landing-stage: Rialto*

Campo San Luca (102/B1)
Situated halfway between St Mark's Square and the Rialto Bridge, this square is the site of trade and shopping, occasionally with stalls. *Landing-stages: San Marco or Rialto*

Campo San Polo (97/E6)
Tree-shaded benches make the biggest Campo in Venice a welcome place to take a break. *Landing-stage: San Silvestro*

Campo Santa Maria Formosa (99/D6)
Steer races once took place where stalls now display appetizing market produce and what passes for antiques. *Landing-stage: San Zaccaria*

Napoleon called St Mark's Square 'Europe's loveliest salon'

Piazza San Marco (102/C2–3)
★ This is probably the most crowded square in Italy. What you can see here is described elsewhere in this guide. St Mark's Square takes on a magic of its own when the shadows grow longer and the setting sun tinges it, touching St Mark's lion to a fiery glow on his column. The square was restored between 1985 and 1991. Despite Mark Twain's acerbic comments to the contrary, Napoleon before him pronounced St Mark's Square 'Europe's loveliest salon'. *Landing-stage: San Marco*

DISTRICTS

Arsenal (104/B–C1–3, 105/D–E1–3)
Arsenale is, strictly speaking, part of the Castello District. However, it doesn't seem at all amiss to treat it as if it were a district in its own right. It is even surrounded by walls. Ships were eased down the Arsenal slipway from the 12th century. At times this was one of the great centres of the medieval and Renaissance European military-industrial complex. Four stone lions crouch before the entrance to the Arsenale, which covers an area of 32 ha. Venetian spoils of war taken from Greece, they signalize that warships were built in the Arsenale. *Landing-stage: Arsenale*

Ghetto (97/D1)
★ The Jewish ghetto (*geto* or *gheto)* is probably an abbreviation of borgetto (small borough or borgo). Jews began to settle in the Cannaregio district, once

the site of metal foundaries, in 1516. It was not long before the city authorities closed the ghetto gates every night to segregate it from Christian neighbourhoods. The Jewish residents of the ghetto were forced to pay the soldiers who guarded the ghetto. In the 17th century as many as 5,000 Jews were living in Venice but today there are only a few dozen. Nevertheless there are kosher shops and a *Museo d'Arte Ebraica* (see the chapter on museums), which is informative on the history of the ghetto. *Landing-stage: San Marcuola*

TOWERS

Campanile di San Marco (102/C3)
★ The Italian word *campanile* is the general term for clock tower but 'the' Campanile means the 98-m-high St Mark's tower to Venetians. Venice is unthinkable without the Campanile. Venetian history seems to be divided into before and after the Campanile fell down on 14 July 1902. The city decided to reconstruct the beloved landmark using the original stones. A decade later, on 12. April 1912, the rebuilt Campanile was inaugurated. You can ascend it by lift to have a superb view across Venice. *Daily 9 am–7 pm (in winter 9 am–4 pm), admission L8,000, landing-stage: San Marco*

Torre dell'Orologio (102/C2)
The clock tower on the north side of St Mark's Square is resplendent in blue and gold, pointing the way to the Venice shopping district, which starts at this corner of the square. One face of the clock in the first storey of the tower is late 15th-century. It indicates hours, phases of the moon and constellations. From the roof, which affords a superb view, if it's open to the public (which it rarely is), two bronze Moors, cast in 1497, strike the hour. *As far as is known to date, the clock tower will remain closed for restoration work till early in 2000, landing-stage: San Marco*

Two bronze Moors strike the hour on St Mark's clock tower. In 1997 they celebrated their 500th anniversary

GONDOLA YARD

Squero di San Trovaso (100/C5)
One of the few working gondola yards in Venice and certainly the most picturesque is in Dorsoduro. The little yard *(squero)* in the Rio San Trovaso still makes the graceful boats by hand. *Landing-stage: Záttere*

Two hours in a museum

The city's museums and art collections attest to centuries of Venetian business acumen and cosmopolitan outlook

No other city can afford to be as matter of fact about possessing world-class art. The tiniest of churches and the grandest of palaces are filled to bursting with paintings and statues for which many a city council would love to endow museums without end. Venice doesn't worry about institutionalizing her art. She wears it proudly. Mark Twain isn't the only scoffer to call Venice a museum and not be entirely wrong at that.

Visitors who plan on coming to Venice and just 'dropping into' a 'museum or two' will soon see that this doesn't make good sense. There are so many museums and their collections are so rich that you have to decide just what you want to see. The Collezione Guggenheim and the superb Galleria dell'Accademia or the Museo Civico Correr and the Biblioteca Nazionale Marciana, the lovely clothes in the Fortuny or the world-famous glass in the Vetrario on Murano – you'll simply have to budget your time.

After deciding, you'll be relieved because then you'll know that you'll be back again to see the ones you missed the first time. The deliberations aren't over with the weighty decision-making process. You have to be patient enough to queue up for an hour or two just to buy a ticket and go into a museum in Venice. If you're spending your holidays here and have enough time, this might not seem daunting but when special exhibitions are mounted, day-trippers, students and Venetians themselves will all be ahead of you in the queue. This isn't the sort of place where museums are merely a refuge from boredom on a rainy day.

Museum opening times vary considerably and this often depends on the number of custodians and other personnel available. You can, however, rely on the accuracy of times given or marked on buildings. Museum ticket prices, and this includes the old charitable foundations

Bookworm heaven: the Biblioteca Nazionale Marciana, here the east façade

called *scuole*, usually cost about L5,000 and, in the case of the Doge's Palace, L17,000. For culture vultures and people who come to Venice several times a year there's a special combined ticket *(biglietto cumulativo)*, valid for twelve months. However, it is only for the Palazzo Ducale, the Museum Correr, the Palazzo Mocenigo, Ca' Rezzonico, Museo del Merletto (Burano) and the Murano Museo del Vetro. The combined ticket is available at participating museums for L17,000.

A reminder about museums. Here, as in most other places, museums tend to be closed one day a week, usually, but not always, on Mondays. Holiday opening hours are usually the same as Sunday opening hours.

Biblioteca Nazionale Marciana (103/D3)
★ If not since Borges, at least since Umberto Eco's world bestseller 'The Name of the Rose' the reading public has been aware of how fascinating old libraries can be. Founded in 1537 by Jacopo Sansovino, the Nazionale Marciana in the Piazzetta San Marco is bookworm heaven. Housing 900,000 volumes, 3,000 incunabula and 13,000 manuscripts, this is one of the major Italian libraries and that's saying something. Scholars beware: the big reading room, which is used every day for study and research, is one of the coldest places in Venice in winter and terribly hot in summer because the heating system is not up-to-date. *Mon–Fri 9 am–7 pm, Sat 9 am–1.30 pm, but only by appointment and with your passports, please, Tel. 04 15 20 87 88, admission free, Piazzetta San Marco, landing-stage: San Marco*

Casa Goldoni (101/E1)
Carlo Goldoni, the famous Venetian playwright or, more accurately, writer of witty comedies of manners, is invariably described as the man who took the masks off actors on the stage 'The mask is always an impediment to a player's acting. If he wants to express joy or sadness, whether he is to be in love or wax wroth, the painted leather is always the same... Nowadays one expects soul from an actor and soul concealed behind a mask is like fire smothered in ashes.' Goldoni's pronouncements are exhibited in the Palazzo Cent'Anni not far from the Canal Grande in San Polo, where Goldoni was born on 23 February 1707 (he died far from home in Paris in 1793). Since 1931 called the Casa Goldoni, the palazzo has housed a theatre museum with memorabilia, costumes, furnishings, manuscripts and editions of Goldoni's work. The playwright spent several years directing plays in his native Venice before going to Paris. The Institute for Theatre Studies is also in this building. *Mon–Sat 8 am–1.30 pm, admission free, Calle dei Nomboli, 2793, landing-stage: San Tomà*

Collezione Peggy Guggenheim (101/F5)
★ 'I would say', was the way Peggy Guggenheim closed her memoirs, tellingly entitled 'Confessions of an Art Addict', in fact she was convinced, that her readers should be more than satisfied with the crop of geniuses pro-

duced by the 20th century and she proceeded to list the usual galaxy: Picasso, Matisse, Mondrian, Kandinsky, Klee, Léger, Braque, Gris, Ernst, Miró, Brancusi, Arp, Giacometti, Lipchitz, Calder, Pevsner, Moore and Pollock. She collected them all and bequeathed them to her beloved Venice when she died in 1979. Duly honoured, the Venetians – presumably without irony – called her 'our last Doge' and buried the American millionairess in the city that was her overriding passion. The art collection one woman succeeded in amassing has remained utterly astonishing. The Guggenheim Collection should be close to the top of any visitor's list. *Wed–Mon 11 am to 6 pm, and frequent special exhibitions, admission L12,000, Palazzo Venier dei Leoni, Dorsoduro, 701, landing-stage: Salute*

Galleria dell' Accademia **(101/E4–5)**

★ This is a central landmark of the Venice cityscape. You reach the Galleria dell'Accademia by crossing the Canal Grande on the Ponte dell'Accademia bridge, leaving the San Marco district and entering terra firma in Dorsoduro. Once you descend from the bridge, the museum looms over you with an orderly queue snaking out in front of the entrance. All these patient people are waiting to see the world's most comprehensive single collection of

MARCO POLO SELECTION: MUSEUMS

1. **Biblioteca Nazionale Marciana**
   Old writings on frail vellum (page 36)
2. **Collezione Peggy Guggenheim**
   What one woman amassed in a lifetime spent with art (page 36)
3. **Galleria dell' Accademia**
   Titian's 'John the Baptist' and other superb paintings (page 37)
4. **Scuola Grande di San Rocco**
   One of the world's most stupendous interiors, decorated by Tintoretto (page 43)
5. **Museo Civico Correr**
   The decline and fall of an imperial republic (page 39)
6. **Museo d'Arte Ebraica**
   Life in the Jewish Ghetto had its pleasant moments (page 39)
7. **Museo Fortuny**
   Commemorates a fashion designer extraordinary (page 41)
8. **Museo Storico Navale**
   A proud naval tradition and victory at sea against the Infidel (page 41)
9. **Museo Vetrario**
   Glass-blowing looks back on a long tradition (page 42)
10. **Pinacoteca Querini Stampalia**
   A Venetian merchant in the Settecento (page 42)

In the spirit of Marco Polo

Marco Polo was the first true world traveller. He travelled with peaceful intentions forging links between the East and the West. His aim was to discover the world, and explore different cultures and environments without changing or disrupting them. He is an excellent role model for the travellers of today and the future. Wherever we travel we should show respect for other peoples and the natural world.

WWF

14th- to 18th-century Venetian painting. All the big names are housed in a building impressively restored by Carlo Scarpa, who restructured the exhibition space. The highlights? There isn't space enough here to list them. Giovanni Bellini's San Giobbe altarpiece in Room 2, Mantegna's 'St George' in Room 4, Giorgione's 'The Tempest' in Room 5, Paolo Veronese's 'The Feast in the House of Levi' in Room 10 and Titian's hauntingly transfigured 'John the Baptist' in Room 6 – the Accademia houses so many masterpieces of Renaissance, Baroque and 18th-century art. Canaletto and Carpaccio – even if you've never been to Venice, it's familiar from Canaletto. *Sun 9 am–8 pm, Mon 9 am–2 pm, Tues–Fri 9 am–9 pm, Sat 9 am–11 pm, admission L15,000, Campo della Carità, landing-stage: Accademia*

Galleria Franchetti (98/A4)

The Ca' d'Oro, a 15th-century palace that was once gilded and now houses the Galleria Franchetti is on your right not far beyond the Rialto arm of the Canal Grande. Even without its gilt stucco, the richly ornate façade reveals something of its former glory in its delicate articulation.

The Galleria Franchetti exhibits its paintings, sculpture, furnishings and carpets from various periods. Not all these treasures are Venetian. Paintings by Mantegna, Titian, Giovanni Bellini, Tintoretto, Tullio Lombardo and Sir Antony van Dyck are hung on two floors of the building. Perhaps the most impressive room of all is the *Sala del Carpaccio*, room 1, which is entered from the Loggia with a view of the Canal. The highlights of this room are Vittore Carpaccio's 'Annunciation' and 'Death of the Virgin'. At the centre of the room stands a remarkably monumental Venetian table – an important 16th-century piece.

A tip: try to visit the Ca' d'Oro on a bright sunny day because the exhibits are shown without benefit of artificial lighting. *Daily 9 am–2 pm, admission L6,000, Ca' d'Oro, landing-stage: Ca' d'Oro*

Icon Museum (103/F2)

The Republic of Venice had a far-flung empire in its heyday, the 16th century, when it ruled Crete, Cyprus and Greece. The magnificent icons in this museum reveal that Venice appreciated the art of her Hellenic subjects. This is Europe's largest collection of Byzantine and post-Byzantine icons from the 14th and 18th centuries. The museum's full name is Museo dell'

Istituto Ellenico di Studi Bizantini e Postbizantini. *Mon–Sat 9 am–12.30 and 2 pm–4.30pm, admission L7,000, Campo San Giorgio dei Greci, 3412, landing-stage: San Zaccaria*

Museo Archeologico (102/C3)
The most important exhibits have come from private collections. The museum collections have been built up over centuries of bequests from Venetian families. In the 16th, 17th, 18th and 19th centuries, Venetian merchants were willing to spend quite a bit on archaeology (or, like English lords, on spoils from conquests). Exhibits include fine Greek Classical and Late Classical statues of women (5th and 4th centuries BC) and the Hellenistic Grimani Altar (1st century BC). *Closed for renovation, Piazzetta San Marco, 52, landing-stage: San Marco*

Museo d'Arte Ebraica (97/D1)
★ Elsewhere in this book the Venetian origin of the ghetto and the Italian etymology of the word from a diminutive for borough has been discussed. The Museum of Hebrew Art is in what was the old ghetto. Recalling Jewish culture in Venice, it does not dwell on the discriminatory treatment meted out to Jews but is instead remarkably upbeat, showing beautiful and interesting artefacts representative of the Jewish contribution to the city. *Daily (except Sat and on Jewish holidays) 9 am–5 pm (in winter till 4 pm, Sun till 5.40 pm) Daily guided synagogue tours between 9.30 am and 3.30 pm), admission L5,000, Campo del Ghetto Nuovo, landing-stage: San Marcuola*

Museo Civico Correr (102/C3)
★ You enter this museum, endowed in 1830 by the rich Venetian Teodor Correr from the west side of the Piazza San Marco, at the farther end of the Procuratie Nuove arcades. The Museo Correr collections afford a marvellous opportunity for enthusiasts to bone up on the rise, heyday, decline and fall of the Venetian Republic. In the very first room the old maps are fascinating. This is where that celebrated Bird's-Eye View of Venice by Jacopo de' Barbari (1497) is kept with the wooden block from which it was printed next to it. A distinguished engraver, de' Barbari spent most of his working life in northern Europe in the service of the Emperor Maximilian and other lesser rulers.

Then come rooms full of paintings. Starting in rooms 10 and 11 with the 14th century, interested observers will notice the growing influence of Flemish painting on 15th-century Venetian art. The interrelationship of Northern and Southern art was promoted by the intensive commercial and trade links between the Netherlands and Venice at that time. In room 15 you can admire one of the museum's great treasures, to earlier art historians and connoisseurs, like the English aesthete John Ruskin, the 'world's greatest painting', Vittore Carpaccio's (1460–1526) 'Dame Veneziane'. Possibly once part of a larger work, it is a representation of two bored-looking ladies with lapdogs and birds. Art historians now tend to resolve the issue of whether these ladies

The Guggenheim Museum is right on the Canal Grande

should properly be called 'Two Courtesans' (because of their low-cut dresses) or whether they are simply bourgeoises by pointing out the platform shoes (showing on the left), worn only by respectable married women at the time.

You can take the best pictures of St Mark's Square from the windows of the Museo Correr. The stairway up to the main floor of the Correr also leads to the *Museo del Risorgimento,* yet another section of this inexhaustible treasure trove of collections. It surveys the end of the proud Republic and the subsequent era, when Austria ruled the islands in the lagoon. *Daily 9 am–7 pm (winter till 4 pm), admission L17,000 (biglietto cumulativo, incl. Palazzo Ducale and other civic museums), Piazza San Marco, landing-stage: San Marco*

Museo Diocesano di Arte Sacra (103/D2)

In the cloister of a 12th-century monastery, liturgical vessels and other appointments taken from churches which have been closed are here on display: chalices, monstrances, codices, tabernacles and banners. There are plenty of important paintings, too, as you've come to expect in Venice: work by Titian, Tintoretto and Gentile Bellini's four organ panels, which used to hang in St Mark's. *Mon–Sat 10.30 am – 12.30, admission free, Chiostro di*

Sant'Apollonia (at the Palazzo Trevisan), landing-stage: San Zaccaria

Museo dell'Estuario (O)
Archaeological finds from the more remote Venetian past are exhibited in this museum on the island of Torcello: artefacts from Altino on the mainland, whence the people who settled on Torcello fled in the 5th century AD before marauding Goths and later the Lombards before they went on to Venice. *Tues–Sun 10.30 am–12.30 and 2 pm–4 pm, admission L3,000, landing-stage: Torcello*

Museo Fortuny (101/F2)
★ Mario Fortuny y Madrazo, a Spanish painter and couturier, came to Venice in 1889, fell under the city's spell and stayed. He became famous for lovely fabrics, designing them himself and making them in his factory on the island of La Giudecca, which still makes Fortuny materials. Aesthetes like the poet Gabriele D'Annunzio and Marcel Proust wore Fortuny bathrobes. Fortuny outfitted ladies of the theatre, among them Eleonora Duse, Sarah Bernhardt and Isadora Duncan.

Fortuny bought a 15th-century palazzo in the San Marco district, which today houses the museum, a monument to the master couturier and fabric designer. The walls are covered in heavy Fortuny materials and bolts of sumptuous cloth are lying about as if awaiting his presence to be measured and cut up to clothe lovely ladies. *Currently closed for renovation, Campo San Benedetto, 3780, landing-stage: Rialto*

Museo del Settecento Veneziano (101/D3)
Dating from the 17th/18th centuries, the Palazzo Rezzonico was built by the architects Baldassare Longhena and (later) Giorgio Massari. It affords the most comprehensive survey of 18th-century Venice, with furnishings, porcelain and costumes, all of them dusty. Unfortunately, the museum is not well kept up. Now that renovation has started, things are sure to change. *Currently closed for renovation, Ca' Rezzonico, landing-stage: Ca' Rezzonico*

Museo Storico Navale (104/B3–4)
★ Two anchors belonging to Austrian battleships captured in World War I, the 'Viribus unitus' and the 'Tegetthoff', guard the entrance, advertising the city's greatest source of pride in her history: the Venetian commercial and naval fleets on which the Republic's astonishing Mediterranean hegemony rested. The museum moved into this building, which was once a granary, in 1961. It houses everything conceivably relevant to maritime history and should delight navy buffs: models and nautical charts, rope and tackle, equipment and lots of marine paintings. The museum's pride and joy is a model bucintoro dating from 1830. The Doges used to be rowed in a bucintoro to the annual ceremony of the Marriage of Venice to the Sea. The original of the bucintoro model was 44 m long and was rowed by 42 men. *Mon–Sat 8.45 am–1.30 pm (Sat till 1 pm), admission L2,000, Riva San Biagio, landing-stage: Arsenale*

Museo Vetrario **(O)**
★ Glass-blowing is recorded from 1000 on Murano. The exhibits in the Palazzo Giustinian are delightfully instructive on the long history of glass-blowing, revealing how imaginative some of these veteran Murano glass-blowers were and how the tradition has been enriched by modern designers. One splendid piece in particular might be singled out among approx 4000 art objects in glass shown: the 15th-century 'Barovier marriage cup' of deep blue enamelled glass. If you're only taking the *vaporetto* to Murano to visit the glass museum and aren't interested in the workshops, which are obviously geared to tourism, you shouldn't get out until it stops at 'Museo' in the Murano Canal Grande. Signs point the way to the glass museum from there. *Thurs–Tues 10 am–5 pm, admission L8,000, landing-stage: Museo*

Pinacoteca Querini Stampalia **(103/D1)**
★ Venetian merchants were extremely prosperous. The Pinacoteca gives a good idea of how luxurious life was in an aristocratic family with a fortune made in trade. Count Giovanni Querini Stampalia lived here and had no heirs. His bequest to the city comprised the palazzo, a library of 200,000 volumes and a collection of paintings which was even more impressive, including works by Bellini, Tiepolo and Pietro Longhi (1702–85), who is not so famous as the luminaries mentioned above yet reveals himself a prolific master of genre painting, an 18th-century speciality made popular in the Netherlands in the 17th century. His sketches of Venetian life are unsurpassed – rich in details which are recognizable today. Twenty of his scenes are hung in the palazzo. *Tues–Sun 10 am–1 pm and 3 pm–6 pm, Fri and Sat till 10 pm, admission L10,000, Campiello Querini Stampalia, landing-stage: San Zaccaria*

SCUOLE

Venice is known for an institution known (plural form) as *scuole*, which translates literally as 'schools' although it means chapter-houses, almshouses and similar charitable foundations, some financed by crafts guilds or even by resident foreigners. Since many of these communal organisations were not lacking in funds,

Three painters at night

Culinary homage is paid nightly in the famous 'Harry's Bar' to Venetian art. The names of Bellini, Titian and Carpaccio are on the drinks list and menu. A Bellini is a cocktail of white peach juice topped up with sparkling prosecco or champagne. A Titian is the same cocktail in Titian red, of course, made with raspberry juice or syrup. Carpaccio is a world-famous snack or hors d'oeuvre consisting of paper-thin slices of raw beef, served with a sauce that remains as well guarded a secret as the recipes for the above cocktails.

they competed in promoting the arts. Consequently, the Doges and members of the *scuole* were public patrons of the arts.

Up to 50 *scuole* were active at any given time. Unfortunately, only a few of these institutions have been preserved with their original furnishings, appointments and decoration. In the following, we shall discuss the four most important *scuole*, which are nowadays very simply art museums.

Scuola Grande dei Carmini **(100/B3)**
The Carmelite Order, which owned this chapter-house, promoted at least one distinguished artist: the painter Giambattista Tiepolo (1696–1770). *Mon–Sat 9 am–1 pm, admission L7,000, Campo dei Carmini, landing-stage: San Basilio*

Scuola di San Giorgio degli Schiavoni **(104/A1)**
As xenophobic as any other people the world over, the Venetians chose to despise Dalmatians – about 200 were resident in the city at one time – as Slavs, in Italian *schiavoni*. Nonetheless, the Dalmatians had their assembly house decorated between 1502 and 1511 by the great Vittore Carpaccio himself, choosing motifs from the lives of the Dalmatian patron saints George, Tryphonius and Hieronymus as the subject of narrative murals and ceiling paintings. Carpaccio applied his usual virtuosity and light hand to the task. *Tues–Sat 9.30 am–12.30 and 3 pm–6.30 pm, Sun 9.30 am–12.30, admission L5,000, Calle dei Furlani, landing-stage: Arsenale*

Scuola di San Giovanni Evangelista **(97/D5)**
Once the chapter-house of the confraternity of St John the Evangelist, this fine building dates from the 13th century. Behind its magnificent Gothic façade the 'Venice Committee' works out strategies for advertising Venice in the US. Don't miss the Renaissance staircase designed in 1498 by Mauro Coducci (Codussi). *Only Sun and Mon 10 am–4 pm, admission L5,000, Campiello San Giovanni, landing-stages: San Tomà or Ferrovia*

Scuola Grande di San Rocco **(100/C1)**
★ The confraternity of St Roch, the patron saint of plague victims was founded in 1478 after plague continued to break out in the city. In 1564 a competition was announced to decorate the interior of the chapter-house. The winner was Jacopo Tintoretto (1518–94). The terms of his contract required him to paint three pictures a year. Tintoretto proved a workaholic who finished 56 paintings, some of them on a vast scale, in 23 years of dedication to the task. A 'Tintoretto Museum', the Scuola is perhaps comparable in scale as an undertaking by one painter only to Michelangelo's Sistine Chapel in Rome, albeit less well known to those who are not art historians. Tintoretto's masterpiece, the 'Crucifixion' he executed in 1565, is in the Sala dell'Albergo on the first floor and on your left. Most of the other paintings are of biblical scenes. *Daily 9 am–5.30 pm (in winter 10 am–4 pm), admission L8,000, Campo San Rocco, landing-stage: San Tomà*

Where to dine

Wherever a Venetian cook is at work, it takes time. Everything served is fresh and a meal has at least three courses

It was one of those rainy days so typical of Venice in mid-October. The water was already standing in stagnant pools on the Piazza San Marco. Soaked through, my shoes were making my socks damp so I fled to a restaurant. It was early, only noon and the waiter had spotted me as what I was, a tourist. Lunch in Venice is rarely eaten before one or, at the earliest, 12.30. The waiter suspected all I wanted was to slurp down some pasta and then rush back out again for more sightseeing. Not until I ordered in Italian, and in the right order, an *antipasto*, for starters, a *risotto* or rice dish as my *primo piatto*, or first course, followed by a *secondo*, as my main course, did my waiter unbend to give me a fleeting smile. However, he was still suspicious, pointing out that my *risotto* would take at least half an hour. I laughed outright and told him, if that were not the case, I'd go right back out into the drizzle because that would mean the food served at his restaurant wasn't worth eating anyway.

The *risotto* did take a good half hour, the *pasta* 15 minutes, the *fagioli* 20 minutes – anyone who's not willing to wait for rice, pasta and beans to be prepared as they should be needn't bother with lunch in Venice – or anywhere in Italy for that matter – because lunch is an important meal here. This doesn't mean that Venetians approach it with solemn reverence. They lunch over lively discussions which make restaurants in which most of the customers are locals hum with the buzz of conversation.

Communication is writ large throughout the day whenever people meet for a meal or a snack. Many Venetians start out the day with a *colazione*, breakfast, in the bar round the corner. Venetians don't go in for large breakfasts anyway. Most are satisfied with a cappuccino and a *brioche*, which is pretty much like its French counterpart. Others prefer a *caffè*, which is what we call a strong black espresso. Tourists should do as the Venetians do and do without fried eggs and ham or bacon for breakfast because otherwise they'll be too full to enjoy some of the treats the day holds in store for them, like *cicheti* or satisfying *tramezzini*, sandwiches eaten with an *ombra* around eleven.

From Canaletto's time: Caffè Florian

A bar is where you go for those. It's high time for your first glass of wine in the form of an *ombra*. With it you eat cheese and sausage titbits, morsels of octopus and squid, meatballs and olives as your *cicheti*, or triangular one-piece sandwiches on white bread, the popular *tramezzini*.

Travellers who want to skip lunch will often find even more tasty little delicacies in a bar. These include *panino*, open-face ham or cheese sandwiches or rolls, eaten warm or cold. Venetians look askance at tourists bringing in their own sandwiches and cans of beer to picnic blearily under the arcades of St Mark's Square, thus clogging the flow of pedestrian traffic and making nuisances of themselves. There is even a city ordinance forbidding this crude practice and police enforce it by approaching 'offenders' with warnings.

A Venetian meal often begins with *sarde in saor*, superb sardines in vinegar and oil, guaranteed to tickle even the most jaded of palates into anticipation of what is to come. You can follow them up with *risotto nero*, creamy rice cooked in squid ink. This is the Greek way of utilizing all that ink, first noted by Horace among parvenu Romans and perfected in Venice. Venice is indeed the perfect place for lovers of shellfish – ranging from *sogliola* (sole or flounder) and *aragosta* (crayfish) to *vongole*, scallops. A plate of *fritto misto di mare*, an array of crisply deep-fried seafood, comes as a revelation to those who have always associated squid and calamari with rubber teething rings.

If you're not into shellfish or even fish, you might like to indulge in offal, something the Venetians know how to cook to perfection. The crowning delight: *fegato alla veneziana*, calves' liver cut into strips and sautéed lightly with onions with a dash of white wine.

Venetians, like most Italians, drink wine with meals. Visitors can usually rely on the house wine, sold by glass or carafe, as *vino della casa*. When this is a good one, waiters have even been known to take offence at requests for the wine list. If you do ask to see it, what you'll find there is wine from the Veneto, especially from the province of Treviso, and Friuli. Sparkling prosecco, beloved in Venice as an apéritif, comes from sites between Valdobbiadene and Conegliano. The grape varieties usually encountered here, as in much of northern Italy, are Pinot, Riesling and Sauvignon blanc and the reds Bardolino, Cabernet and Merlot. Italian wine regulations distinguish between three qualities: modest *vino da tavola*, table wines, D. O. C. (Denominatione di Origine Controllata) wines with at least a distinctive regional style and top-level D. O. C. G. wines of guaranteed regional origin. Italy has been in the throes of a wine revolution for over a decade and many young, experimental vintners refuse to bow to the dictates of the wine regulations – as a result, their exciting wines must be labelled merely as *vino da tavola*, although they are anything but that.

Before we go into individual restaurants, a suggestion: be sure

MARCO POLO SELECTION: RESTAURANTS

1 **Antico Calice**
Where Venetians like to lunch (page 50)

2 **Antico Martini**
Serves food until midnight (page 48)

3 **La Caravella**
International clientele, regional cuisine (page 48)

4 **La Zucca**
Hearty food served on scrubbed designer tables (page 53)

5 **Al Ponte del Diavolo**
Well worth crossing to Torcello for (page 49)

6 **Da Fiore**
Mara Zanetti's desserts are heavenly (page 49)

7 **Poste Vecie**
Below the fish market, fish as you'd expect (page 49)

8 **La Colomba**
Classic cuisine and an arty ambience (page 48)

to leave enough room for dessert! Venetians are world-class bakers, renowned for cakes, biscuits and sweet fritters of all kinds.

BARS/CAFÉS/ICE-CREAM PARLOURS

Causin **(100/C2)**
It's well worth looking for this café because it serves what is probably the best – made of course on the premises – ice-cream in Venice. Natives of the city queue up with the rest to enjoy its creations. *Mon–Sat from 10 am, Campo Santa Margherita, 2996, landing-stage: Ca' Rezzonico*

Chioggia **(103/D3)**
Right across from the Doge's Palace you can escape the tourist crush to the piazzetta, the lobby of St Mark's Square as it were, and watch everyone being jostled and stepped on. This *caffè*, which means what it says, a coffee-house, is noticeably less grand and certainly not so dusty as the neighbouring *Florian* and *Quadri* under the arcades on St Mark's Square, both of them world-renowned and rather forbidding. The weather permitting, a pianist plays in the Chioggia. *Daily from 9 am, Piazzetta San Marco, 8–12, landing-stage: San Marco*

Florian **(102/C3)**
After Canaletto featured it in his vedute, Balzac and Mark Twain both sat here, right on St Mark's – and of course it's expensive. *Thurs–Tues from 9.30 am, Piazza San Marco, 56/59, landing-stage: San Marco*

Nico **(101/D6)**
This ice-cream parlour is on the Záttere with a view of the island of La Giudecca. The ice-cream is superb, with a range including exotic flavours. In summer

especially, Venetians like to soak up the sun on the broad pavement. There are two more good caffès near Nico: *Aldo* and *Cucciolo. Fri–Wed from 10 am, Záttere ai Gesuati, 922, landing-stage: Záttere*

Sacro e Profano **(98/B5)**
Spicy sausage and *vino,* cheese and *pane ...* and great atmosphere at the bar or the three or four tables. Ideal for a snack or a drop to drink in between sights. *Daily at noon and in the evening till midnight, Ruga degli Orefici/Sottoportici, 502, landing-stage: Rialto*

Ai Stagneri **(98/C6)**
☺ This is where you can enjoy breakfast with the Venetians or take a break from shopping in the San Marco district. The young proprietors serve what are probably the best, certainly the most imaginative, open sandwiches, *panini,* in Venice. *Mon–Sat 7 am–9 pm, Calle degli Stagneri/ Calle delle Fava, 5246, landing-stage: Rialto*

Vino Vino **(102/A3)**
Delicious morsels that don't cost the earth – the ideal place to drop into for between-meal snacks or a pleasant chat over a glass of – for such reasonable prices superb – wine. *Wed–Mon 10.30 am–midnight, Calle delle Veste, 2007, landing-stage: Giglio*

Al Volto **(102/A1)**
☺ Don't be afraid to go into this *enoteca,* wine-bar. It's nearly always packed and (this argues well for what you'll find), with Venetians. *Mon–Sat 10 am–2.30 pm and 5 pm–10.30 pm, Calle Cavalli, 4081, landing-stage: Rialto*

RESTAURANTS CATEGORY 1

(At least a three-course meal for one person including drinks for over 80,000 lire)

Antico Martini **(102/A3)**
★ Opera at its finest will waft – let's hope once again in the not all-to-distant future – across from La Fenice, tragically gutted by fire in 1996. Emilio Baldi's imaginative cuisine is a perfect match for this operatic setting. *Closed Wed noon and Tues, Campo San Fantin, 1983, Tel. 04 15 22 41 21, landing-stage: Giglio*

La Caravella **(102/A3)**
★ Venetians don't really care so much for this restaurant because its maritime decor seems rather stylized. However, it's popular with seafood addicts from everywhere else – Spanish and Portuguese visitors seem to swear by it – because it serves the best fish in Venice, albeit at rather salty prices. There's a pleasant bar where you can wait for a table and smoke, if you're so inclined, because this is a non-smoking restaurant. *Open daily, Calle Larga XXII Marzo, 2397, Tel. 04 15 20 89 01, landing-stage: Giglio*

La Colomba **(102/B3)**
★ One of the great experiences in Venetian gastronomy and just two minutes' walk from St Mark's Square. Guests are spoiled here – for a price naturally – with classic culinary sophistication and lavish spreads. The walls are sumptuously decorated with dozens of paintings, prints and collages by distinguished artists. *Closed Wed, Piscine di Frezzeria,*

1665, Tel. 04 15 22 11 75, landing-stage: San Marco

Corte Sconta **(104/A2)**
Not easy to find and unpretentiously furnished, this restaurant offers much, much more than meets the eye, with a superb range of fish dishes. The kitchen is up to anything demanding. The proprietress is inclined to rattle off the carte du jour in briskly confidence-inspiring Italian since there is no written menu. Our suggestion: trust the chef and order an opulent dégustation spread. One warning, though: quality doesn't come cheap! *Sun and Mon closed, Calle del Pestrin, 3886, Tel. 04 15 22 70 24, landing-stage: Arsenale*

Da Fiore **(97/E5)**
★ Once a wine tavern, this restaurant has been built up by a very enterprising and pleasant young couple into a superb seafood restaurant (coquilles St Jacques with thyme and fish ravioli), a groaning cheese board and exquisite deserts. Since 1996 this extraordinary restaurant has been awarded a Michelin star. *Sun and Mon closed, Calle del Scaleter, 2202, Tel. 041 72 13 08, landing-stage: San Silvestro*

Montin **(100/C4)**
Fed up with fish and hankering after something else for a change? Then why not try some succulent *fegato alla veneziana*, a far cry indeed from Gary Larson's liver and onions. And the setting is historic. This is where the great Eleonora Duse had Wagnerian trysts with the flamboyant Gabriele D'Annunzio. *Tues evenings and Wed closed, Fondamenta delle Eremite, 1147, Tel. 04 15 22 71 51, landing-stage: Ca' Rezzonico*

Al Ponte del Diavolo **(O)**
★ This restaurant on the island of Torcello has successfully challenged the far more famous Locanda Cipriani. Gourmets know this without being told. Dishes are prepared with fresh garden vegetables from the island. Open at noon! *Evenings and Thurs closed, Torcello, 10, Tel. 041 73 04 01, landing-stage: Torcello*

Poste Vecie **(98/A4)**
★ Right behind Hemingway's fish market a little bridge and six steps lead down into this venerable, but enchanting, really Venetian restaurant. Fish straight from the market is magically transformed from the Expressionist palette of pink and grey that awed the Colonel. In the old days you couldn't just drop in and hope to find an unoccupied table. Things have changed and now you can. You'll even be greeted by the strains of Vivaldi, so pervasive in Venice, and a glass of prosecco. If you're still up to it after a lavish meal, ask to have the sumptuous dessert trolley rolled up to your table. *Tues closed, Pescheria, 1608, Tel. 041 72 18 22, landing-stage: Rialto*

RESTAURANTS CATEGORY 2

(A meal with several courses for one person, including drinks for 50,000 to 80,000 lire)

Antica Birraria La Corte **(97/E5)**
Opened in 1999 in an old brewery at the northern tip of idyllic Campo San Polo, this is the place for serious foodies who don't

need any extra trimmings at lunch or dinner. The décor of the lofty and narrow rooms and covered courtyard, is astringently cool and chic in keeping with the consummate yet understated craftsmanship displayed in the kitchen. Specialities: grilled chicken, pizzas, veal and even horse meat. You drink your apéritif at tables outside in the square. *Mon closed, Campo San Polo, 2168, Tel. 04 12 75 05 70, landing-stage: San Silvestro*

Antico Calice **(98/C6)**
★ ◉ The 'Antique Chalice' is one of those fabulous places you wonder whether you should keep to yourself so they won't be spoiled or overrun – it would be such a pity to find yourself crowded out on your next trip to Venice. If you're curious about the workings of the kitchen, don't hesitate to make reservations at one of the seven tables right in front of it! It's advisable to make reservations in any case – especially if you want to eat between 1 pm and 2 pm – so you won't be disappointed. It's less crowded in the evenings. *Closed Sun evening and Mon, Calle degli Stagneri, 5228, Tel. 04 15 20 60 84, landing-stage: Rialto*

Da Arturo **(102/A2)**
Again an old wine tavern, converted into an exceptional restau-

Pleasure alla veneziana: a canal-side table

rant. Unusual for Venice, Ernesto serves only meat dishes – sophisticated and imaginative creations. The accompanying salads are bouquets of ingredients not always associated by pedestrian minds with such uses. *In Aug closed Sun, Rio Terrà Assassini, 3656, Tel. 04 15 28 69 74, landing-stage: Sant'Angelo*

Fiaschetteria Toscana **(98/C5)**
There aren't many places you can banquet so sumptuously in Venice. From goose liver to zabaione, San Daniele ham to risotto, steaks done sensitively to your liking (Mark Twain was appalled at what happened to steak in Venice in his day) and sautéed fish: the chef invites you to a convito, a gourmet's symposium. Elegantly unostentatious, reasonable prices. *Tues closed, Salizzada San Giovanni Crisostomo, 5719, Tel. 04 15 28 52 81, landing-stage: Rialto*

La Furatola **(100/C3)**
The proprietor doesn't worry about keeping up appearances. If the fish doesn't look fresh enough at the market, he just closes up shop and basta! When the place is open, the food is fabulous and satisfyingly simple. Over 30 types of grappa are on tap and the *zabaione caldo*, hot, foamy sabayon made with marsala, is the best you'll find in Venice. *Closed Thurs, in Jan and Aug also Tues, Calle Lunga San Barnaba, 2870a, Tel. 04 15 20 85 94, landing-stage: Ca'Rezzonico*

Al Graspo de Ua **(98/B6)**
If you're patient enough, you'll find it, in a tiny alley off the Campo San Bartolomeo. You'll be rewarded for your efforts with good Venetian home cooking. *Closed Mon, in July and Aug also Tues, Calle dei Bombaseri, 5094, Tel. 04 15 20 01 50, landing-stage: Rialto*

Harry's Dolci **(O)**
This was supposed to become a sweet shop and patisserie on La Giudecca. However, once again the king of Venetian gastronomy, Cipriani, became carried away and went further than originally planned. Now it's a remarkably good restaurant, right on the Canale della Giudecca, reasonably priced by Cipriani standards. *Closed Tues and Nov to Mar, Fondamenta San Biagio, 773, Tel. 04 15 22 48 44, landing-stage: Sant' Eufemia*

Vini da Gigio **(98/A3)**
Excellent food and always based on what is in season and fresh. The décor is sparkling and pleasantly simple, with reasonable prices to match. Outstanding value for your money. Be careful: it's so popular you'll have to make reservations here! *Closed Sun evening and Mon, Fondamenta San Felice, 3628a, Tel. 04 15 28 51 40, landing-stage: Ca'd'Oro*

RESTAURANTS CATEGORY 3

(Several courses for one person including drinks for less than 50,000 lire)

All'Antica Mola **(97/E1)**
A picture-book trattoria – simple and cosy with typical hearty Venetian fare (lots of fish, vegetables and a robust wine from the barrel). Weather permitting, guests sit behind in the little garden or in front on the Canal.

Open daily, Fondamenta dei Ormesini, 2800, Tel. 041 71 74 92, landing-stage: Guglie or Sant'Alvise

Bandierette **(99/E5)**
Good home cooking. Workers come here to eat lunch, with a choice of one, two or three *primi* and *secondi* courses. The à la carte fare is much more lavish in the evening – mostly fish dishes. No wonder you have trouble finding a table here. *Sun closed, Barbaria delle Tole, 6671, Tel. 04 15 22 06 19, landing-stage: Ospedale*

Alla Madonna **(98/A5)**
If every other eatery in Venice is packed, don't despair. You'll still probably manage to find a table

Shrines to Venetian cuisine

Danieli **(103/E3)**
A luxury hotel with a marvellous lobby and a magnificent roof terrace where you dine with spectacular views of the island of San Giorgio Maggiore and the Lido. From L140,000. *Open daily, Riva degli Schiavoni, 4196, Tel. 04 15 22 64 80, landing-stage: San Zaccaria*

Do Forni **(103/D2)**
This is where tycoons have their business lunches. Heads of state, kings and the most prominent members of the international jet set eat here. You eat off silver, the glasses are what they should be and the waiters are in livery. More importantly, the food is top-quality and the wines come from the world's leading sites. From L100,000. *Open daily, Calle Specchieri, 468, Tel. 04 15 23 21 48, landing-stage: San Zaccaria*

Harry's Bar **(102/C4)**
The name does not just include the famous bar; the first-floor restaurant, too, is an institution. This is where Giuseppe Cipriani invented the Vero Carpaccio, raw beef shaved paper-thin with a world-beating sauce made according to a recipe successfully kept secret. If the restaurant is too expensive for you, do have a drink at the bar even though the dry martinis are no longer conjured up in shakers before your eyes as they used to be when Ernest Hemingway was a regular here. From L110,000. *Open daily, Calle Vallaresso, 1323, Tel. 04 15 28 57 77, landing-stage: San Marco*

Quadri **(102/C2)**
The famous caffè in St Mark's Square has an incredibly elegant 1st-floor restaurant. The views of the Piazza and the Campanile are spectacular and the superb food is both Venetian and international, in short, for the discriminating palate because it's consistently the best of everything. Guests come here expecting to be transported to the 19th-century in a romantically sumptuous setting. From L90,000. *Open daily, Piazza San Marco, 120, Tel. 04 15 22 21 05, landing-stage: San Marco*

in the venerable 'Madonna', which has room for 220 guests. Despite its size, it's been popular with Venetians for over 30 years with a deserved reputation for serving tasty, hearty home cooking. *Wed closed, Calle della Madonna, 594, Tel. 04 15 22 38 24, landing-stage: Rialto*

Osteria da Alberto **(99/D4)**
Andrea Tomasella's tenure is fairly recent. He specializes in superbly fresh seafood. *Sun closed, Calle Giacinto Gallina, 5401, Tel. 04 15 23 81 53, landing-stage: Fondamenta Nuove or Rialto*

Rosticceria **(98/C6)**
The perfect spot for a snack or quick meal on the run with *Primi* and *secondi* courses as takeaway. *Mon closed, Calle della Bissa/Campo San Bartolomeo, 5424, Tel. 04 15 22 35 69, landing stage: Rialto*

Trattoria Alle Vignole **(O)**
A beautiful excursion by vaporetto (no. 13 line) will take you to the island of Vignole. After a refreshing walk through market gardens, you can eat a delicious meal here in an enchantingly rural setting. Self-service and cheap, a varied menu featuring hearty fare. *Mon closed, Isola delle Vignole, Tel. 04 15 28 97 07, landing-stage: Vignole*

La Zucca **(97/E3)**
★ With its bare wooden designer tables, this restaurant has rather a Japanese feeling about it. The food served here is, however, hearty Venetian home cooking, with local specialities like toasted bread with herring for starters or duck braised in prosecco as your main course. What is particularly satisfying is the wide selection of casserole dishes. Vegetables figure prominently, especially *la zucca*, courgettes. *Sun closed, Ramo del Megio, 1762, Tel. 04 15 24 15 70, landing-stage: San Stae*

ETHNIC COOKING

Gam-Gam **(97/D1)**
Good kosher cooking with an Israeli-Italian touch. Sample the *tahina* a try and don't overlook the gefilte fish and the excellent Israeli wines! *Fri closed, Sottoportego del Ghetto vecchio, 1122, Tel. 041 71 52 84, landing-stage: Guglie*

Sahara **(98/A1)**
The Republic of Venice looked towards the Levant. Why not follow in Marco Polo's footsteps and eat your way eastward? Arab food like *schawarma, cous-cous* or *baba ghannough* is delicious and a real bargain at that! Open until 2 am. *Closed Mon evenings, Fondamenta de la Misericordia, 2519, Tel. 041 72 10 77, landing-stage: San Marcuola*

PIZZERIA

Due Colonne **(97/E5)**
For initiates: probably the best pizzeria in Venice. Speciality: big wheels of pizza dough encrusted with ham and horse meat *(sfiaceti)*. *Sun closed, Campo San Agostin, 2343, Tel. 04 15 24 06 85, landing-stages: San Silvestro or San Stae*

Al Profeta **(100/B3)**
One of the oldest traditional pizzerias in Venice. A decided plus: a delightful garden. *Wed closed, Calle Lunga San Barnaba, 2671, Tel. 04 15 23 74 66, landing-stage: Ca' Rezzonico*

MADE IN ITALY
Murano
VENEZIA

Shopping with style

Compare prices. You'll need walking shoes for the expensive Venice shopping district

Two things are remarkable about Venice as a place to shop. First, most small shops look to the unwary as if they offered permanent discounts. Second, you'll be tempted by the shop-window displays to spend more than you really can afford. Taken together, these two factors make Venice a hot spot indeed for inveterate shoppers because, whatever else you may say about it, the pearl of the lagoon is expensive. After all, the Venetian Republic made its money in trade and commerce, starting with haberdashery.

Between St Mark's Square and the Rialto Bridge the haberdashers or mercers, hence *mercerie*, once had their shops. Their wares were sold throughout the maze of alleys in this district. From humble beginnings merchants rose to the heights of the silk trade and the elegant boutiques which are such a hazard for visitors on first arriving in Venice.

This El Dorado, where gold changes hands – migrating from seller to buyer in a dizzying daily turnover – begins below the clock tower on the north side of St Mark's Square. The streets leading off from this point remind you of the origins of all this visible wealth since their names start with Merceria: *Merceria dell' Orologio, Merceria di San Zulian, Merceria San Salvador* and *Merceria II Aprile*. There is one shop after another here and boutiques line the long *Calle Larga XXII Marzo* on the west side of St Mark's Square, which is, if anything, even more upmarket than the north side.

In the triangle formed by the east side of St Mark's Square, the Accademia Bridge to the west and the Rialto Bridge to the north, determined shoppers will find anything the heart desires: old books and young cheese, hand-made shoes and exquisitely fine fabrics, the noblest of aged vinegars and cold-pressed olive oil, pasta and bread of all kinds, sizes and shapes, marbled papers and free-blown glass, this last often kitschy as kitsch can be and just waiting to lure shopping addicts to binge on it and break it.

You'll soon realize that the best bargains are to be had in shoes. The reason for this is the shoe leather Venetians themselves wear out in traversing their city. The average Venetian

The Murano glass-blowers are world-famous – kitsch and art rub shoulders here

MARCO POLO SELECTION: SHOPPING

1. **Cassini**
Old books and old vedute at reasonable prices (page 56)
2. **Farmacia di San Polo**
A paradise for herbalists with herbs and herbal tinctures (page 59)
3. **Il Fornaio**
Pasta for those first nostalgic meals at home (page 58)
4. **Il Papiro**
Fine marbled paper is versatile and fashionable (page 59)
5. **La Fonte dell'Olio**
Oil and vinegar from all over Italy (page 57)
6. **Rialto Market**
Fishmongers tout the sea's bounty (page 59)
7. **Ricordi**
Musical instruments made as they always have been (page 60)
8. **Toletta**
Literature and books on Venetian art at rock-bottom prices (page 57)
9. **Valli**
Brocade and batiste – bolts of beautiful cloth (page 61)
10. **Zaggia Claudia**
Valuable old clothes make a comeback (page 57)

spends two hours a day walking. Consequently, shoes, with the exception of the footwear tantalizingly displayed in the best boutiques, have to be reasonably priced.

Shop opening hours in Venice are flexible, generally adapted to the rhythm of life in this fast-paced city. On weekdays – and, as elsewhere in Italy, this includes Saturdays because people work on Saturdays – shops are usually open between 9 am and 12.30 and again from 3.30 pm till 7.30 pm. If you're just spending a weekend in Venice and your plane is due to leave on Monday morning, a word of caution is in order. Shops are closed on Monday mornings so you'll have to do your shopping on Saturday.

ANTIQUES

Of course Venice can no longer draw on what long seemed an inexhaustible store of riches to supply the world with antiques. They are now being brought in from all over Italy. A lot of this stuff is at best old tat or simply worthless junk. Nevertheless, there are a few reliable antiques dealers who sell beautiful old things.

Cassini **(102/B3)**
★ This is perhaps the best antiquarian bookseller in Venice, dealing in books and prints. *Calle Larga XXII Marzo, 2424, landing-stage: San Marco*

Scarpa **(101/D4)**
The owner of this shop is a knowledgeable antiquarian and

connoisseur of drawings and Old Master paintings. *Accademia, 1022, landing-stage: Accademia*

Zaggia Claudia **(100/C3)**
★ This is the place for well preserved old toys, Venetian pearls, stylish costume jewellery and even some notable Art Nouveau and Art Déco dresses in superb condition. *Calle de Casin, 1195 a, landing-stage: Ca' Rezzonico*

PICTURE FRAMES

Picture frames, *cornici*, look back on a long tradition here. They are often still laboriously handcrafted in small workshops which continue to use techniques handed down from the days of the Doges.

Bearzi **(97/D1)**
Picture frames are meticulously restored and touched up with gilt here in the old Jewish ghetto. *Campo Ghetto Vecchio, 1154, landing-stage: San Marcuola*

Canestrelli **(101/F5)**
The restorer also has his own flea market selling a welter of old frames so take time to pick over them. *Campiello Barbaro, 364, landing-stage: Salute*

BOOKS

Emiliana **(102/B2)**
Stock includes a wide range of books – in German and other languages too – on Venice. *Calle Goldoni, 4487, landing-stages: Rialto or San Marco*

Fantoni **(102/A-B1)**
Probably the best selection in Venice of books, and not just Italian ones, on art, architecture and photography. *Salizzada San Luca, 4121, landing-stage: Rialto*

Toletta **(101/D4)**
★ The best address for bargains (also in languages other than Italian) in literature and art books on art and literature. *Calle della Toletta, 1214, landing-stage: Accademia*

DELICATESSENS

In this most sensuous of all cities, it isn't surprising that you'll come across small and even tiny shops selling *specialite gastronomiche*, delicatessens with everything for the gourmet. Travellers who haven't been spoilt all their lives with such culinary delights (and sights!) will probably be overwhelmed simply by what they find at the corner grocer's. Now for some suggestions on what you can and should stock up on to take home with you as a special treat:

Aliani **(98/B5)**
The entire universe of Italian cheeses for your delectation with a focus on northern Italian greats (Gorgonzola, Taleggio, Parmesan, Grana ...). *Ruga Rialto, 654, landing-stage: Rialto*

La Fonte dell'Olio **(103/E2)**
★ Italy produces vintage olive oils designated like wines by region and site. Be sure you really do buy *olio extra vergine di oliva*: only cold-pressed, 'virginal' oil is worth carrying all the way home for a salad. *Calle San Provolo, 4963, landing-stage: San Zaccaria*

Il Fornaio **(102/B1)**
★ ☺ You've never dreamt that there could be so many variants on the theme of pasta as this Land of Cockayne displays. Before you become hopelessly involved, remember that your purchases, made on the premises, will become dry and brittle with time. *Calle San Luca, 4579, landing-stage: Rialto*

Mauro el Forner de Canton **(98/A3)**
Biscotti, bruschette, brigiolini... a cornucopia of sweet and savoury biscuits. *Strada Nova, 3845, landing-stage: Ca'd'Oro*

Panificio Colussi **(102/A2)**
☺ This is the sort of bakery you'd like to take home with you, lock, stock and barrel, bread, rolls, twists, biscuits and all. *Calle della Mandola, 3726, landing-stage: Sant' Angelo*

Rizzo **(98/C5)**
Sustenance for your sweet tooth: honey. *Salizzada San Giovanni Crisostomo, 5778, landing-stage: Rialto*

Volpe **(97/D1)**
This bakery shop specializes in kosher bread and traditional Jewish pastries. It's where you might expect it to be located: in what was once the Jewish ghetto. *Campo Ghetto Vecchio, 1143, landing-stage: San Marcuola*

PRESENTS

Bac Art Studio
It's not always easy to find just the one, the perfect present for those you've left back home. You certainly don't want to insult the recipients of your conscience-stricken bounty by loading them down with kitsch – and lovely things have their price the world over. You might try the etchings and aquatints with charming scenes of Venice sold in two branches of the Bac Art Studios. **(101/F3)**: *Campo San Maurizio, 2663, landing-stage: Giglio;* **(98/B5)**: *Ruga Rialto, 1069, landing-stage: Rialto*

C'era **(98/A6)**
Candles are always nice and melt down anyway. What about a light right from the Canal Grande? *Riva del Vin, 1098a, landing-stage: San Silvestro*

Minima Libraria **(102/A4)**
In this extraordinary shop Ettore Sobrero sells miniature books in bookcases and miniature desks. Enchanting toys for adult collectors – and expensive: these minimalist works of art are hideously expensive – costing up to three million lire. *Calle delle Ostreghe, 2436, landing-stage: Giglio*

GLASS

Barovier & Toso **(O)**
If you feel you owe it to yourself to visit the glass-blowers' island of Murano, limit yourself to two old family businesses where you're most likely to find free-blown glass and traditional pieces. These families are inextricably entwined with the history of Murano. *Fondamenta dei Vetrai, 28, Murano, landing-stage: Colonna*

L'Isola **(102/B3)**
Carlo Moretti refuses to follow the trend and spew out the kitsch

artefacts which overflow into most glass shops in Venice and Murano. His handsome glasses and bowls are compelling pieces of modern design. *Campo San Moisè, 1468, landing-stage: San Marco*

HERBAL MEDICINES

Farmacia di San Polo **(97/E6)**
★ The tradition of *erbe medicinali* goes back to ancient times in Venice. Every reputable pharmacy has a section selling herbal medicines. One of the best, with inexhaustible stocks of herbs and herbal tinctures, is the Farmacia di San Polo. *Campo San Polo, 2012, landing-stage: San Silvestro*

PÂTISSERIES

Marchini **(101/F3)**
A marvellous place to lose count of calories. Speciality: delicate puff-pastry boats with subtle creme fillings. *Calle del Spezier, 2769 (near Campo San Stefano), landing-stage: Giglio*

Rosa Salva **(102/B1)**
The classic patisserie for the discerning sweet tooth (and connoisseurs of cappuccino). *Campo San Luca, 4589, landing-stage: Rialto*

MARKETS

Campo San Barnaba **(100/C3)**
This 'market' is a one-man show entirely. He comes up the Rio di San Barnaba canal and ties up his boat, only to vanish in a bevy of Venetian housewives all bent on buying the best in fresh market produce. *Tues–Sun mornings, landing-stage: Ca' Rezzonico*

Rialto Market/ Pescheria **(98/A-B4-5)**
★ ☺ The oldest market in Venice starts right behind the Rialto Bridge on the San Polo side. It's been in operation since 1097. The district was once a hub of finance. Now no less commercially minded, stalls display luscious fruit and vegetables, spices and herbs, meat, poultry and lots of fish and shellfish. At the end of the market on the Campo Pescheria, you'll come across the city's biggest fish market with the freshest fish of all. Twice daily except Sun. *Landing-stage: Rialto*

MARBLED PAPERS

That familiar yet enduringly elegant marbled paper, hand-printed in Venice for centuries, has become fashionable again in recent years. Two pioneering shops let you watch it being made: ★ *Il Papiro* **(101/F3)**, *Campo San Maurizio/Campo San Stefano, 2764, landing-stage: Giglio; Alberto Valese-Ebru* **(101/F3)**, *Campo San Stefano, 3471, landing-stage: Giglio*

MASKS

Two mask-makers whose creativity places them head and shoulders above the crowd: *Tragicomica* **(101/E1)**, *Calle dei Nomboli, 2800, landing-stage: San Tomà; Marega* **(101/D1)**, *Campo San Rocco, 3046a, landing-stage: San Tomà*

FASHION

Of course all the great Italian designers like Armani, Biagiotti, Cerruti, Dolce & Gabbana, Krizia, Missoni and Valentino are represented with their collections in Venice too – many of them in their own shops – because you can't think of Italy without thinking fashion. All the fashion boutiques are, without exception, north or west of St Mark's Square in the main shopping streets.

Laura Crovato (101/E3)
A highly unusual little shop where you can hunt to your heart's content for second-hand dresses, silk scarves and costume jewellery. *Calle delle Botteghe, 9225, landing-stage: San Samuele or Sant'Angelo*

Mandich (97/E1–2)
Reassuringly posh clothes for him and her. *Rio Terrà Farsetti, 1412, and diagonally across from it, landing-stage: San Marcuola*

Top Ten (102/B2)
On an incline, young fashion guaranteed to appeal. *Calle Goldoni, 4487a, landing-stages: Rialto or San Marco*

Valeria Bellinaso (97/F6)
Witty and elegant hats, scarves, bags and gloves, all made of silk. *Campo Sant'Aponal, 1226, landing-stage: San Silvestro*

MUSIC

Nalesso (101/F3)
Specialists in Venetian Baroque music (CDs, cassettes, scores). *Calle del Spezier, 2765d, landing-stage: Giglio*

Ricordi (101/F2)
★ 🚶 Music students buy their sheet music here. There is also a superb selection of traditionally crafted string instruments – as well as a remarkably comprehensive record collection of 17th, 18th and 19th-century Venetian music. *Calle dello Spezier, 2765, landing-stage: Sant'Angelo*

JEWELLERY

Al Canale (98/B5)
Exciting modern ceramic costume jewellery fashioned in all shapes, sizes and colours. *Ruga Rialto, 973, landing-stage: Rialto*

Missiaglia (102/C3)
Once jewellers to the Italian royal family, this is still the very best, *the* jewellery shop in Venice. *Piazza San Marco, 125, landing-stage: San Marco*

SHOES & LEATHER GOODS

La Corte delle Fate & Silvia (99/D6)
Two shops located diagonally across from each other, each selling lovely, stylish shoes. *Salizzada San Lio, 5540 und 5690, landing-stage: Rialto*

Nevada (98/A–B5)
One of many good places in the city for reasonably priced leather jackets, with a particularly wide selection. *Ruga dei Spezieri, 233, landing-stage: Rialto*

Segalin (102/B2)
✪ If your feet swell from all that walking in Venice so your shoes pinch, the only thing to do about it is to go to Segalin and have a pair custom-made. Regular customers are kept on file so they can order these extravagant shoes even from

abroad. *Calle dei Fuseri, 4365, landing-stage: Rialto*

TOYS

La Casa Storta (101/D1)
Quirky toys from granny's magic toy shop, ranging from tin cars to hand-sewn dolls. *Calle Larga, 2768 (close to Campo San Tomà), landing-stage: San Tomà*

Signor Blum (100/C3)
Those unmistakably Venetian three-dimensional wooden puzzles. *Campo San Barnaba, 2840, landing-stage: Ca' Rezzonico*

LACE/EMBROIDERY

Old and new *pizzi e ricami* are on sale round St Mark's square. Be careful. Prices are sky-high and it's even advisable to bargain for some of these frothy wares.

Maria Mazzaron (103/E2)
Connoisseurs of bobbin lace think she's the best in Venice and convinced that she's justifiably renowned – if you don't mind paying the prices she asks. *Fondamenta dell'Osmarin, 4970, landing-stage: San Zaccaria*

MATERIAL

Bevilaqua (103/D2)
This shop in an alley behind St Mark's looks back on a long tradition. Old pieces of cross-stitch embroidery and tapestries, including Gobelins, are sold here. *Calle di Canonica, 337 b, landing-stage: San Marco*

Valli (102/B3)
★ Bolts and bolts of brocades and batiste in lovely colours, a dress-maker's dream. *Calle Morosoni de la Regina o dei Pignoli the corner of Parrogia di San Moisè, 783, landing-stage: San Marco*

DEPARTMENT STORES

Coin (98/C5)
Salizzada San Giovanni Crisostomo, 5787, landing-stage: Rialto

Standa (102/B1)
Campo San Luca, 4540, landing-stage: Rialto

Lace is pretty and pretty expensive, too

DANIELI

A good night's sleep

Wherever you stay in Venice and whatever you pay – you'll sleep within old walls

No matter what time of the year you come to Venice, it's almost impossible to find affordable accommodation if you haven't booked well in advance. Therefore, the first thing to do is book your hotel before you leave home. Further, if you book by telephone, be sure you have written confirmation of your booking. Finally, take advantage of cheaper combination rail or flight tickets with city transport.

Because *vaporetto* lines run so frequently, you do have the option of staying on the mainland, perhaps at the industrial port of Marghera or in the industrial suburb of Mestre, and going to Venice during the day. However, if you do so, you'll miss a great deal of the charm of Venice. It's only when day-trippers have left, that there's enough room for you to stroll through the city at leisure without being distracted by your fellow visitors.

The best (and most expensive) hotels in Venice – apart from the Cipriani on La Giudecca and luxury accommodation on the Lido – are clustered around St Mark's Square. They all boast views of the Canal Grande even though the view – take it philosophically as Venetians do! – may in fact be across a sea of roofs.

Hotel and inn rooms have usually undergone frequent and regular restoration and renovation. The Venetians know that if they let everything fall down, they'll be killing the goose that lays the golden egg. Tourism is the main source of revenue in Venice and tourists are catered to here. For this reason, many rooms even have cable television so that you can watch programmes in your own language.

Room prices do not usually include breakfast on the B & B principle. Since hotel breakfasts are usually far too expensive with the standard coffee, croissants, butter and jam, it's a good idea to give them a miss and go to the nearest bar – that's much more fun anyway. You'll be breakfasting with Venetians and have the feeling that you're really here after all.

We have classified hotels below according to price in three groups and give the lowest and top price for a double room with bath in each price category to show the full price range. The minimum prices given by hotel

Sheer luxury: Hotel Danieli

proprietors themselves turn out to be only for off-season accommodation in the cheapest room available in a particular hotel. Venetian hoteliers do tend to be extraordinarily flexible, if not casual, about prices as listed – demand nearly always exceeds supply. Nor is Venice ever really off-season as far as the tourist trade is concerned. Even if you arrive on a rainy January morning in the middle of the week, you can expect to find prices of 50 per cent and more above the minimum listed. It may be worth your while to ask about a discount *sconto*, especially if you're planning to stay for several nights.

HOTELS IN CATEGORY 1

(luxuriously appointed double room without breakfast from approx 300,000 a night)

Des Bains **(O)**
★ This fine Belle Époque hotel is popular even when the Film Festival is not on. It is on the Lido, set in grounds which are extensive by Venetian standards. *Mid-Nov to mid-March closed, 193 rooms and suites, L550,000–830,000, Lungomare Marconi, 17, Tel. 04 15 26 59 21, Fax 04 15 26 01 13, landing-stage: Lido*

Cavalletto e Doge Orseolo **(102/C2)**
A stylish hotel behind the old arcades on the north side of the Piazza San Marco. Reasonably priced indeed, when you consider its prime location with a view of the gondolas in the Bacino Orseolo. *95 rooms, L300,000 to 550,000, Calle del Cavalletto, 1107, Tel. 04 15 20 09 55, Fax 04 15 23 81 84, landing-stage: San Marco*

Concordia **(102/C2)**
Boasting all modern amenities, this hotel is right behind the Piazza San Marco clock tower. *57 rooms, L310,000–650,000, Calle Larga San Marco, 367, Tel. 04 15 20 68 66, Fax 04 15 20 67 75, e-mail concordia@doge.it, landing-stage: San Marco*

Europa e Regina **(102/B4)**
Located right on the Canal Grande, with spacious single rooms and beautiful suites. *192 rooms and suites, from L550,000–1,100,000, Calle Larga XXII Marzo, 2159,Tel. 04 15 20 04 77, Fax 04 15 23 15 33, e-mail gbaroncelli@eittsheraton.com, landing-stage: Giglio*

Metropole **(103/F3)**
The rooms are individually decorated, some of them furnished with antiques, which enhance the charm of this hotel as a historic building; it was used in the 18th century as a granary. Although close to St Mark's Square, it even has a delightful little garden. *72 rooms, L330,000–740,000, Riva degli Schiavoni, 4149, Tel. 04 15 20 50 44, Fax 04 15 22 36 79, e-mail hotelmetropole@venere.it, landing-stage: San Zaccaria*

Monaco & Grand Canal **(102/C4)**
This elegant hotel also has an excellent restaurant as well as really superb views across and down the Canal Grande. *71 rooms, L340,000 to 850,000, Calle Vallaresso, 1325, Tel. 04 15 20 02 11,*

MARCO POLO SELECTION: HOTELS

Fax 04 15 20 05 01, e-mail mailbox @hotelmonaco.it, landing-stage: San Marco

Principe **(96/B3)**
★ This is the perfect hotel for travellers who come by train. You can walk to the station and save the vaporetto fare. Despite the location, its rooms are quiet. *128 rooms, L350,000–480,000, Lista di Spagna, 147, Tel. 041 71 50 22, Fax 041 71 90 61, landing-stage: Ferrovia*

Sofitel **(96/B5)**
Surrounded by one of the few green parks in Venice, this hotel is exceptionally quiet even though it's close to the train station and the Piazzale Roma bus terminal. *97 rooms L460,000 to 650,000, Giardino Papadopoli, Santa Croce, 245, Tel. 041 71 04 00, Fax 041 71 03 94, landing-stage: Piazzale Roma*

HOTELS IN CATEGORY 2

(comfortable medium-range, double room without breakfast between approx 170,000 and 300,000 lire a night)

Accademia – Villa Maravegie **(101/D4)**
★ The name of this hotel near the Galleria dell'Accademia means literally 'Villa of Marvels'. The most marvellous thing about it is its beautiful garden, which ensures blissful peace and quiet. Its clientele is not ostentatious, tending instead to be here for the art. *27 rooms, L200,000–345,000 including breakfast, Fondamenta Bollani, 1058, Tel. 04 15 21 01 88, Fax 04 15 23 91 52, landing-stage: Accademia*

Luxury hotels in Venice

Bauer **(102/B3–4)**
This hotel offers several advantages. First, three minutes' walk through two gates takes you to the Piazza San Marco. Second, there's a gondola stop right at the entrance. Third, when you leave the hotel you are on the relatively quiet square in front of the church of San Moisè. *198 rooms and suites, L430,000–1,300,000, Campo San Moisè, 1459, Tel. 04 15 20 70 22, Fax 04 15 20 75 57, landing-stage: San Marco*

Cipriani **(O)**
Sheer luxury! The ultimate in grand Venetian hotels. Founded by the legendary hotelier Giuseppe Cipriani, the hotel that bears his name was once a dock. A magnet for the rich and beautiful of this world, the Cipriani boasts the only private pool at the centre of the city. The hotel operates its own boat shuttle service round the clock from the hotel on the island of La Giudecca to the Molo of St Mark's. *Nov–Mar closed, 78 rooms and suites, L875,000–1.750,000, Giudecca, 10, Tel. 04 15 20 77 44, Fax 04 15 20 39 30, e-mail cipriani@gpnet.it*

Danieli **(103/E3)**
No other hotel has seen so many distinguished guests come and go. One famous couple retains a room which most hotels wouldn't have on the books: room no. 13. In 1832 George Sand and Alfred de Musset stayed in this very room when they were having an affair. The handsome hotel lobby is famous. Mere mortals can enjoy it by having a cup of coffee there while big-name hunting in this elegant setting. *237 rooms and suites, L600,000–1,350,000, Riva degli Schiavoni, 4196, Tel. 04 15 22 64 80, Fax 04 15 20 02 08, landing-stage: San Zaccaria*

Excelsior **(O)**
Famous during the Belle Époque for fabulous parties, the Excelsior is still a favourite with the rich and royalty. On the Lido, it has its own superbly kept up private beach. *197 rooms and suites, L660,000–930,000, Lungomare Marconi, 41, Tel. 04 15 26 02 01, Fax 04 15 26 72 76, landing-stage: Lido*

Gritti Palace **(102/A4)**
This magnificent 16th-century palazzo belonged to the Doge Andrea Gritti. Now it lodges the international jet set. The terrace facing the Canal Grande was Jean Cocteau's idea of 'the most beautiful place in the world' and he wasn't far wrong. *93 rooms and suites, L590,000–1,600,000, breakfast included, an exception in this range, Campo Santa Maria del Giglio, 2467, Tel. 041 79 46 11, Fax 04 15 20 09 42, landing-stage: Giglio*

La Calcina **(100/E6)**
If you're looking for the personal touch with individually decorated rooms and spectacular views of La Giudecca, this small hotel is the perfect place for you to stay. *29 rooms, L180,000–280,000, Záttere, 780, Tel. 04 15 20 64 66, Fax 04 15 22 70 45, landing-stage: Záttere*

Carpaccio **(101/E1)**
The Palazzo Barbarigo, in which this hotel is housed, is located in a quiet part of the city yet affords views of the Canal Grande. *13 rooms, L220,000–330,000 including breakfast, Calle Corner, 2765, Tel. 04 15 23 59 46, Fax 04 15 24 21 34, landing-stage: San Tomà*

La Fenice et des Artistes **(102/A3)**
★ If you stay here, you'll be right where everything's going on. The hotel is situated in the maze of alleys where the elegant shops and reputable antique dealers are. The complex consists of four palazzi with a lovely courtyard garden. *65 rooms and suites, L170,000–380,000 including breakfast, Campiello della Fenice, 1936, Tel. 04 15 23 23 33, Fax 04 15 20 37 21, landing-stage: Giglio*

Flora **(102/A3)**
True to its name, this delightful hotel boasts a small but beautiful flower garden in the midst of a sea of houses. *44 rooms, L205,000–340,000 including breakfast, Calle Larga XXII Marzo, 2283a, Tel. 04 15 20 58 44, Fax 04 15 22 82 17, landing-stage: Giglio*

Gabrielli Sandwirth **(104/A3)**
★ ☀ If you're fourtnate enough to have a front room, you'll have magnificent views out across the island of San Giorgio and the Molo of San Marco. *105 rooms, L250,000–620,000, Riva degli Schiavoni, 4110, Tel. 04 15 23 15 80, Fax 04 15 20 94 55, landing-stage: Arsenale*

Kette **(102/B3)**
Elegant and quiet due to its location, this hotel is notable for its spacious rooms. It is as close as it can be to La Fenice, soon to be restored to its former glamour. *56 rooms, L200,000 to 360,000, Piscine San Moisè, 2053, Tel. 04 15*

Theatre and opera luminaries stay at the Fenice

20 77 66, Fax 04 15 22 89 64, landing-stage: Giglio

Savoia e Jolanda **(103/E3)**
Book as far in advance as possible because you want a room with a balcony on the top floor with the same breathtaking views as the luxurious Danieli Hotel but at a much more reasonable price. *59 rooms, L180,000–350,000, Riva degli Schiavoni, 4187, Tel. 04 15 20 66 44, Fax 04 15 20 74 94, landing-stage: San Zaccaria*

Villa Mabapa **(O)**
★ Owned by the Best-Western chain, this hotel affords tempting views of the lagoon from the Lido. Built in the 1930s, this hotel started out as a very comfortable mansion. *61 rooms, L190,000–420,000, Riviera San Nicolò, 16, Tel. 04 15 26 05 90, Fax 04 15 26 94 41, e-mail mabapa@mbox.vol.it, landing-stage: Lido*

HOTELS IN CATEGORY 3

(just the basics but comfortable enough, double room without breakfast between approx 100,000 and 250,000 lire a night)

Abbazia **(96/B3)**
★ One wing of an 18th-century monastery still inhabited by Carmelite monks has been converted into a hotel. Very peaceful and friendly. *39 rooms, L150,000–330,000 including breakfast, Calle Priuli detta dei Cavalletti 66/67, Tel. 041 71 73 33, Fax 041 71 79 49, landing-stage: Ferrovia*

Canaletto **(98/C6)**
A small hotel living up to a big name at the heart of the shopping district. *17 rooms, L70,000–300,000, Campo San Lio, 5487, Tel. 04 15 22 05 18, Fax 04 15 22 90 23, landing-stage: Rialto*

Guerrato **(98/B5)**
★ An unpretentious but well kept up *albergo* is housed in a building 800 years old. The rooms are unusually bright and spacious for Venetian lodgings. Some afford picturesque views of the green grocers' market. *15 rooms, L120,000–180,000, Calle dietro la Scimia, 240a, Tel. 04 15 22 71 31, Fax 04 15 28 59 27, e-mail hguerrat@tin.it, landing-stage: Rialto*

Iris **(101/D1)**
★ Cheap – one of two Frari churches close by. *29 rooms, L100,000–220,000, Campo San Tomà, 2910/A, Tel. and Fax 04 15 22 28 82, e-mail htiris@tin.it, landing-stage: San Tomà*

Do Pozzi **(102/A3)**
When you leave the quiet inner courtyard and step into the street, you're amazed to find that you're right in the midst of all the hustle and bustle. Works by contemporary painters are hung in the rooms and halls. *29 rooms, L150,000–280,000, Calle Larga XXII Marzo, 2373, Tel. 04 15 20 78 55, Fax 04 15 22 94 13, landing-stage: Giglio*

La Residenza **(104/A2)**
Book ahead to stay at this Gothic palazzo; there aren't many rooms. *14 rooms, L150,000–240,000, Campo Bandiera e Moro, 3608, Tel. 04 15 28 53 15, Fax 04 15 23 88 59, landing-stage: Arsenale*

Alla Salute da Cici **(102/A5)**
★ Right in Dorsoduro but lots of village atmosphere. Just the place for art lovers: the Galleria dell' Accademia and the Collezione Guggenheim are only a few minutes' walk from here. *50 rooms, L130,000–200,000, Fondamenta Ca'Balà, 222, Tel. 04 15 23 54 04, Fax 04 15 22 22 71, landing-stage: Salute*

Wildner **(103/E3)**
In a location worthy of a luxury hotel, this one has some rooms with the same beautiful views but at a much lower price. *16 rooms, L100,000–300,000, Riva degli Schiavoni, 4161, Tel. 04 15 22 74 63, Fax 04 15 26 56 15, e-mail wildner@veneziahotels.it, landing-stage: San Zaccaria*

FOR YOUNG PEOPLE

Istituto Canossiano **(O)**
Open all year round, this is an inexpensive hostelry where only girls can stay. It has two big dormitories with a total of 35 beds (L22,000 without breakfast). *Giudecca, Ponte Piccolo, 428, Tel. 04 15 22 21 57, Landing-stage: Palanca*

Youth Hostel **(O)**
The youth hostel *(ostello per la gioventù)* on the island of La Giudecca can sleep 260 people at once and has 60 single-sex rooms. To stay here you must have a Youth Hostel organisation membership card. Open all year round. An overnight stay with breakfast costs L24,000. *Admittance only between 6 pm and 11 pm, Ostello A. I. G., Fondamenta Zitelle, 86, Tel. 04 15 23 82 11, Fax 04 15 23 56 89, landing-stage: Redentore*

Summer accommodation
During the summer months the following cheap accommodation is available for young people: *Convento San Francesco della Vigna* **(O)**, *Tel. 04 15 22 24 76, landing-stage: Celestia; Domus Civica* **(96/B5)**, *Calle delle Sacchere, 3082, Tel. 041 72 11 03, landing-stage: San Tomà*

Commissario Brunetti investigates

Her passion for opera led to her first bestselling novel. When Donna Leon attended an opera rehearsal at La Fenice in the 1980s, the man at her side vowed he could 'murder the conductor!' 'I'll do it for you in a novel,' she is said to have replied. Not long afterwards she sat down at her desk and Commissario Guido Brunetti sprang from her inventive brain all set to solve this difficult case, in the novel 'Venetian Finale', which has sold more than 700,000 copies since 1992. By now the American bestseller author has lived in Venice for twenty years with six more exciting and intelligently written crime novels to her credit, all of them set in Venice. In them she touches on current social issues and develops the atmospheric possibilities of background to the fullest. Her clever and circumspect Italian detective is regarded by a growing host of fans worldwide as a worthy successor to Simenon's Maigret.

Venice diary

Venice is the most festive city in the world, a magical setting for exciting events: holidays and highlights

An early description of Carnival, penned by an expert: 'I stopped before a comely Arlecchina, took her roughly by the hand and compelled her to dance a minuet with me. Everyone laughed and willingly made room for us. My Arlecchina was an accomplished dancer ...' Walking through Venice, you can easily imagine how the legendary philanderer Giacomo Casanova must have plunged into Carnival festivities. In his day and ours the Venice year begins with Carnival. Carnival had declined until tourism managers in the late 1970s revived it with the support of the city authorities. It certainly is no longer the light and airy masquerade of the Middle Ages, when barbers were princes and Doges gondoliers.

Yet the Venetian Carnival has survived to inaugurate the year once again. This is, after all, the ideal setting for public festivities.

Religious holidays like Christmas and Easter are not the only important dates in the events calendar. Venetians are still so proud of their Republican past that they continue to celebrate the Marriage of Venice to the Sea (with the historic regatta). On a completely profane level, they are culture enthusiasts, jubilantly lionizing all the modern artists and especially the film stars and famous directors who come to the bi-annual art Biennale, the annual Venice Film Festival and the theatre and architecture festivals. In Venice you can find out all you need to know about the various festivals from the *Ente Autonoma la Biennale di Venezia* **(102/B3–4)**, *Ca' Giustinian, San Marco, 1364 a, Tel. 04 15 21 87 11, landing-stage: San Marco*

Historic vessels participate in the Regata Storica

PUBLIC HOLIDAYS

1 January *(New Year's Day)*; 6 January *(Epiphany)*; Easter Sunday and Monday; 25 April *(Independence Day)*; 1 May *(Labour Day)*; 15 August *(Assumption Day)*; 1 November *(All Saints)*; 8 December *(Immaculate Conception)*; 25 and 26 December *(Christmas and Boxing Day)*.

Many museums are closed on public holidays although some mounting special exhibitions stay open then. Shops and restaurants are not forced to close. It's up to them when they want to be open and they all have their own ideas about opening hours, which vary considerably as a result.

SPECIAL EVENTS

January

In the early morning on 1 January Venetians meet on the shores of the Lido to usher in the New Year in the right spirit: *capodanno in spiaggia* (New Year on the beach) with snacks and hot drinks. There are always a few hardy souls, *ibernisti*, who take their first – brief – swim of the year.

On Epiphany older people, strictly speaking that includes anyone over 50, dress up as witches and row for their very lives on the Canal Grande. During the *Regata delle Befane* a huge witch's stocking dangles from the Rialto Bridge.

Gothic carnival revived for fun and tourism

MARCO POLO SELECTION: EVENTS

1 **Su e Zo per i Ponti**
People huffing and puffing up and down the bridges (page 73)

2 **Vogalonga**
A popular regatta for all oar-propelled boats (page 74)

3 **Festa del Redentore**
Walk accross to La Giudecca on pontoons (page 75)

4 **Regata Storica**
An historic procession through the Canal Grande (page 75)

February/March

Masks appear sporadically in the streets of Venice by mid-January but the officially revived version of the Gothic festival, *Carnevale*, is confined to the last eleven days before Ash Wednesday. During those two weeks festivities are at their height in and around Piazza San Marco. This period marks the beginning of the tourist season so by February hotel rooms are only to be had at peak-season prices. On Shrove Tuesday evening Carnival ends symbolically with the burning of Pantalone at the stake (the commedia dell' Arte practice that derives from the burning of Judas). Then, music lovers, still masked, proceed along the Riva degli Schiavoni to the church of Santa Maria della Pietà, where the traditional *Ash Wednesday Concert* begins at the stroke of midnight.

March

Every second Sunday the city marathon takes place, known as ★ *Su e Zo per i Ponti*, an endearing event which translates literally as 'up and down the bridges', an apt title indeed. The route goes from the Ponte della Paglia, the little bridge on the Molo in front of the Doge's Palace and on through all six districts before circling back to Piazza San Marco.

March/April

A memorable experience is the *benedizione del fuoco*, the 'Blessing of the Fire', which takes place in the late afternoon on the Thursday before Easter in St Mark's Cathedral. The high point of the Easter week liturgy, it starts with the church completely dark and culminates in the lighting of thousands of candles.

April

25 April: Once a holiday commemorating Italian liberation, this day has declined to something like Valentine's Day. The custom has developed of presenting one's wife or girl friend with a rose or, finances permitting, a piece of gold jewellery on the *Festa di San Marco*.

May/June

On Ascension Day Venice celebrates the *Festa della Sensa*, the ceremonial marriage of Venice in the person of the Doge to the Sea. The rites go back to 1000

AD, when a Venetian fleet sailed away to conquer Istria and Dalmatia, thus securing Venetian supremacy in the Adriatic and marking the beginning of the Republic's hegemony in the Mediterranean. The Doge used to cast a wedding ring into the sea inscribed with the words 'We marry thee, our sea, as a sign of real and permanent rule'. The mayor performs this symbolic task at a ceremony with city dignitaries on the Lido. On the Sunday just before or after Ascension Day (careful: the dates are often changed!) the ★ ⚙ *Vogalonga* takes place, a regatta in which every oar-propelled boat in the city may participate. It goes from the Molo at St Mark's Square past the islands of Vignole, Sant'Erasmo and San Francesco del Deserto, through the canals of Burano and Murano, through the Canale Cannaregio and back down the Canal Grande to St Mark's Square.

Another event which takes place in May or June but only every four years (2003, 2007) in the Basin of San Marco is the *Palio delle Antiche Repubbliche Marinare,* a regatta in which four galleys, representing the ancient Italian sea powers of Amalfi, Genoa, Pisa and Venice, compete against each other. Hundreds of people in historic costume line the pavements.

In the last week of June an enjoyable festival with a big lottery takes place in *San Pietro di Castello,* or more accurately, on the lawn in front of the Patriarch's old Cathedral. Wine flows freely and

There's always a quiet place to stand and watch the festivities

local specialities are eaten to the great delight of visitors.

June–October

Every two years (2000, 2002) the *Art Biennale* takes place with exhibitions of contemporary art at major venues throughout the city.

July

On the third Sunday in July relief from the plague epidemic of 1576 is commemorated at the ★ ☥ *Festa del Redentore.* A pontoon bridge is run across to the island of La Giudecca from the Záttere for a thanksgiving procession to the church of the Redentore. The most important part of the festival takes place the night before. Venetians take to lantern-decorated boats on the Giudecca canal, with picnics, drinking and music on the water. The whole thing is pretty and lots of fun. At midnight fireworks light the sky. Young people continue on to the ☥ Lido to celebrate until the sun rises over the lagoon.

August/September

For ten days in late August and early September, the Lido is the venue of the famous *Mostra Internazionale del Cinema.* Along with the French film festival in Cannes, this is the world's most important film festival.

September

The first Sunday in September is reserved for the ★ ☺ *Regata Storica,* perhaps the most colourful Venetian festival of them all. A procession of historic boats – with their crews in the costume appropriate to their vessel – on the Canal Grande makes Venetian maritime glory come alive again. Afterwards gondoliers and other professionals stage the traditional gondola regatta from the St Mark's Molo. If you want to be in Venice at this time, you'll have to book a room months in advance, especially one with a view of the Canal Grande.

On the third Sunday in September, Burano is the place to be for the local *Fish Festival,* especially if you like seafood. The main event is a rowing-boat regatta.

In September there is also a *Contemporary Music Festival* with concerts by leading orchestras and soloists.

October

On the first Sunday in October, the island of Sant'Erasmo throws a big *Wine Festival.* Music, dancing and lots of food and drink are what it's all about except for a rowing-boat regatta in which both men and – it's unique in this respect – women pull the oars. A week later the starting pistol goes off in Stra on the Brenta Canal for the *Venice Marathon.*

November

On 21 November the ☺ *Festa della Salute,* the most important festival in memory of the plague, is celebrated in a markedly religious framework. Like the Festa del Redentore, this one, too, goes back to a plague vow. Between Santa Maria del Giglio and the Chiesa Santa Maria della Salute a pontoon bridge spans the Canal Grande, permitting people to go across to the church and light a candle commemorating deliverance from the terrrible epidemic of 1630–31, when a third of the population of the city and the islands died.

Out on the town

Venice doesn't close down at night. There's lots to do and see

When the sun sets and darkness envelops the streets, the bridges and squares, Venice looks as if she's early abed. The impression is deceptive and one that has persisted for centuries yet this, in a way, is a good thing. Obviously Venice isn't the place for aficionados of discos, bar brawls and clubs. However, it doesn't hurt to remember that it wasn't until he had seen Venice after dark that Mark Twain succumbed to the city's magic. When all the modern day-trippers have departed, another city, one with the population of a town, emerges with a different pulse and rhythm.

During the tourist season especially, and that means from March to October and again during the ten days of Carnival, there's quite a bit going on in the evenings. First of all, there are three theatres (for which a good knowledge of Italian is necessary, particularly if you want to appreciate Goldoni comedies in dialect at the Goldoni), and five cinemas showing good films, quite a few in English. Second, and this is not surprising in the city Vivaldi worked in all his adult life, writing not only instrumental music but, as he boasted in 1739, 94 operas (although only 50 are known), concerts are given in scuole, palazzi and churches. The Pietà, where he taught, still devotes many evenings to his music. On a more mundane level, the celebrated casino and a handful of discos are open late. In recent years, pub crawlers will be relieved to note, bars and pubs, artists' cafés and jazz cellars have sprung up where young people visiting the city can make the acquaintance of local students and all the American Junior-Year-Abroaders and European students spending a memorable year in Venice. On summer evenings, there's music in the squares.

In short, only a disgruntled tourist hungry for standard consumer culture fare or philistines addicted to the universal bar scene might consider nights boring here. For one thing, so many writers have been enchanted with Venice over the past three

In the evening when the day-trippers are gone, Venice displays her charms

centuries that this might be your chance to put in some cosy reading. Come equipped to do so or buy whatever your budget allows on arrival. This is the place for nocturnal walks – particularly on misty autumn and winter evenings – if the archetypal horror conjured up by Roeg hasn't made you afraid to step outside your lodgings once the sun sets.

BACAROS AND OSTERIE

These are cosy but simple wine bars, rather like pubs, in which Venetians feel at home chatting and playing cards, snacking (or occasionally eating a meal), washed down by the usual *ombra,* or glass of white wine. There are a great many bacaros and what follows is simply a short list of places which are an attractive option for extending an evening beyond the evening meal or for having a midday or evening meal if you prefer to eat something light and enjoy the local ambience while doing so. We recommend:

All'Arco **(98/A5)**
Imaginative sandwiches that include toasted open-face varieties. *Mon–Sat 8 am–4 pm and 6.30 pm–10 pm, Calle dell'Arco, 436, landing-stage: Rialto*

Antico Dolo **(98/A5)**
The place seats only about a dozen guests but you find unusual delicacies here like pumpkin gnocchi with sage leaves, polenta and dried fish, toasted open vegetarian sandwiches and garlic bread. A speciality is *trippa rissa,* tripe. *Mon–Sat 10 am–3 pm and 6.30 pm–10 pm, Ruga Vecchia San Giovanni, 778, landing-stage: Rialto*

Al Buso **(98/B4)**
Night owls can linger at this bacaro longer over a snack and a glass or two of wine because it's open until after midnight. *Thurs–Tues 10 am–1.30 pm and 5 pm–1 am, Calle delle Pegola, 2281, landing-stage: Ca'd'Oro*

Candela del Bomba **(98/B4)**
Snacks at the bar and really tasty *primi. Tues–Thurs 10.30 am–10.30 pm, Calle del Forno, 4297, landing-stage: Ca'd'Oro*

Do Mori **(98/A5)**
Like an ancient pub, this *bacaro* near the Rialto fish market is over 500 years old. It's the oldest of its kind in Venice. Pots and copper kettles hang from the ceiling and, more importantly, more than 100 outstanding wines await you at the bar. There's a wide selection of triangular sandwiches *(tramezzini)* and other snacks. *Mon–Sat (except Wed noon) 8.30 am–1.30 pm and 5 pm–8.30 pm, Calle dei Do Mori, 429, landing-stage: Rialto*

Osteria al Milion **(98/C5)**
This wine bar is another ancient one, one of the city's oldest, and it comes to life in the evening. It is crowded into a court in which Marco Polo's family house is said to have been. In the spirit of the great traveller, this is the place for trying out your Italian and striking up a conversation with Venetians. The buffet snacks are always fresh and tasty. *Thurs–Tues from 6 pm, Corte del Milion, 5841, landing-stage: Rialto*

Ai Promessi Sposi **(98/B4)**
★ Well seasoned hors d'oeuvres *(cicheti)* at the bar and all sorts of delicious variations on the theme of fish. *Thurs–Tues 9.30 am–3 pm and 5 pm–11 pm, Calle dell'Oca, 4367, landing-stage: Ca' d'Oro*

Do Spade **(98/A5)**
During the day workmen come here and in the evening the place is a favourite with students. Cosy, with panelling and good, inexpensive food, good wines from Friuli and the Veneto. *Mon–Sat (except Thurs afternoon) 9 am–2.30 pm and 5 pm–11 pm, Calle Do Spade, 860, landing-stage: Rialto*

Ai Vini Padovani **(101/D3)**
Hidden away in an alley, this is a good place to sample excellent local fare. The young, friendly proprietors serve a variety of *cicheti*, sausages with mushrooms or *cotechino* (hearty sausage served warm) with polenta, a delicious staple; and outstanding wines. *Mon–Fri 9 am–8 pm, Calle dei Cerchieri, 1280, landing-stage: Ca' Rezzonico*

DISCOS

Acropolis **(O)**
This is where rich kids let off steam when they're holidaying on the Lido with their parents. As you might expect: expensive! *Summer Thurs–Sat 9 pm–4 am, winter only during Carnival, Lungomare Guglielmo Marconi, 22, landing-stage: Lido*

King's Club **(O)**
🚶 Because it's so close to the airport, DJs don't spare the decibels or your eardrums. Young people come over here from Marghera and Mestre. *Sat from 11 pm, Sun 3 pm–7 pm, Via Ca' Zorzi, 2, Tessera, the no. 5 bus line from Piazzale Roma stops almost at the door*

Piccolo Mondo by El Souk **(101/D4)**
Artists sometimes look in here because it's so close to the

MARCO POLO SELECTION: ENTERTAINMENT

1. **Ai Promessi Sposi**
   Great ambience in a *bacaro* with good wine (page 79)
2. **Campo San Polo**
   In summer the square is turned into an open-air cinema (page 82)
3. **Da Codroma**
   Where students love to meet for conversation and live music (page 81)
4. **Linea d'Ombra**
   Cocktails with a more spectacular view? Nowhere! (page 81)
5. **Palazzo del Cinema**
   If you must go to a film in Venice, go here (page 80)
6. **Paradiso Perduto**
   Young jazz lovers throng to 'Paradise Lost' (page 81)

Galleria dell'Accademia. *Tues–Sun 10 am–8 pm (pub) and 10 pm–4 am (disco), Calle Contarini Corfù, 1056 a, landing-stage: Accademia*

THE CASINO

The Venice Casino is in two places but not at once. In winter it's right on the Canal Grande in the handsome Palazzo Vendramin-Calergi, where Richard Wagner died in 1883. In summer it's on the Lido where the jet set is. It closes down in the first two weeks of October and April. Be careful here, because the stakes start high so it's obviously out of bounds for most. At the roulette tables you have to part with – in winter – at least L25,000 for a single jeton. The casino is open from 3 pm. Associated with both the summer and winter casinos are the city's most elegant and expensive nightclubs.

Winter Casino with nightclub Casanova (**97/E2-3**) *daily 3 pm–3 am, Palazzo Vendramin-Calergi, landing-stage: San Marcuola*

Summer Casino with nightclub La Perla (**O**) *daily 4 pm–3 am, Lungomare Marconi, 4, landing-stage: Casinò*

Information: Tel. 04 15 29 71 11

CINEMA

When it's been pouring for days and high-water warnings are out, it might not be a bad idea to spend an evening at the movies. Since soundtracks are usually dubbed in (except during the Film Festival in late August/early September), here's a chance for you to catch up on your Italian listening comprehension. However, Richard Gere and Julia Roberts somehow don't seem all that convincing in Italian.

The seven cinemas are scattered about the city so it may mean quite an excursion to reach one. You can find out what's on by ringing 198 or the individual cinemas if your telephone Italian's up to it. Otherwise you can look in the local dailies.

Accademia **(101/D4)**
Closed in summer, Calle Contarini Corfù, 1019, Tel. 04 15 28 77 06, landing-stage: Accademia

Astra **(O)**
Via Corfù, 9, Tel. 04 15 26 02 89, landing-stage: Lido

Centrale **(102/B3)**
Piscina Frezzeria, 1659, Tel. 04 15 22 82 01, landing-stage: San Marco

Nazionale **(96/B3)**
Only in summer, Rio Terrà Lista di Spagna, Tel. 041 71 52 65, landing-stage: Ferrovia

Palazzo del Cinema **(O)**
★ *Piazzale del Casinò, Tel. 04 15 26 01 88, landing-stage: Casinò*

Ritz **(103/D 2)**
Calle Larga San Marco, 617, Tel. 04 15 20 44 29, landing-stages: San Marco or San Zaccaria

Rossini **(102/B1)**
Campo San Luca, 4000, Tel. 04 15 23 03 22, landing-stage: Rialto

TRENDY /AFTER MIDNIGHT

Il Caffè **(100/C2)**
✝ Very popular with young locals, this café looks out on to one of the

city's most charming squares. Yummy *tramezzini* and *panini*. In summer live open-air jazz, blues, folk music etc. *Mon–Sat 7.45 am–1.30 am, Campo Santa Margherita, 2963, landing-stage: Ca' Rezzonico*

Cantina Vecia Carbonera (97/F2)
Good jazz, good wine, good snacks – ranging from Parma ham to smoked fish. Thurs and Sun live jazz and Latin rhythms. *Tues–Sun 5 pm–2 am, Rio Terrà della Maddalena, 2329, landing-stage: San Marcuola*

Al Cherubino (102/A1)
Right in San Marco, not far from church of San Luca, but this bar is one of the few to stay open in the wee hours. Frequented by students and pretty young things. *Daily 10 am–1 am, Calle San Antonio, 4118, landing-stage: Rialto*

Da Codroma (100/A3)
★ This is one of the very few places in Venice where live music is seriously cultivated. That's why it's usually crowded with earnest students. *Fri–Wed 7 pm–1 am, Mon–Wed, Fri also 10.30 am–4 pm, Fondamenta del Soccorso, 2540, landing-stage: San Basilio*

Devil's Forest Pub (98/C6)
A genuine English-Irish pub right in the heart of lively San Marco, where you can play darts or backgammon and will often be treated to live music in the evenings. *Tues–Sun 10 am–1 am, Campo San Bartolomeo, 5185, landing-stage: Rialto*

Fiddler's Elbow (98/A3)
Exclusively Irish. All sorts of whisky. Wed and Sat evenings live Celtic music with your pint of stout. *Closed Wed in off-season, Calle del Pistor, 3847, landing-stage: Ca' d'Oro*

Linea d'Ombra (102/A6)
★ The ideal place to spend those soft summer evenings: a bar piano, sophisticated cocktails, good food and enchanting views of La Giudecca and San Giorgio Maggiore. *Thurs–Tues 8 am–2 am, Sun only at noon, Punta della Dogana, 19, landing-stage: Salute*

Martini Scala (102/A2)
With the inducement of quite respectable piano music, this annex of the gourmet restaurant *Antico Martini*, serves snacks even after midnight. Night owls congregate here when everything around has shut down. *Wed–Mon 10 pm–3.30 am, Calle Caffetier, 1980, landing-stage: Giglio*

Paradiso Perduto (97/F1)
★ This bar is a favourite with young people and students who are jazz enthusiasts. Frequent live music. *Thurs–Tues 7 pm–2 am, Sun also 11 am–3 pm, Fondamenta della Misericordia, 2540, landing-stage: Ca' d'Oro*

Torino a Notte (102/B1)
Only three minutes' walk from St Mark's Square: cooling long drinks, snacks and hot music (Wed live jam session). *Tues–Sat 8 am–8 pm and 10 pm–2 am, Campo San Luca, 459, landing-stage: Rialto*

In addition, all the big hotels have bars, among them the Gritti Palace, the Monaco & Grand Canal and the Bauer-Grünwald, with piano music. If you're in the

Life goes on in streets and squares day and night in Venice

mood, any of these might be the sort of place for a – certainly not cheap by any standard – nightcap.

SQUARES

Young people in Venice have always enjoyed taking a ghetto blaster with a tape deck to group gatherings in the city squares. For many years two have shared top billing: *Campo San Luca* (**102/B1**) and *Campo San Bartolomeo* (**98/B–C6**). In recent years the Venezia da vivere organisation has made successful efforts at revitalizing life in the squares. You can now spend summer evenings enjoying live music and street art in the following squares: the *Campi Santa Margherita, Santa Maria Formosa, San Barnaba* and *Santi Giovannie Paolo*, a really pleasant way to while away the hours. *(updates on performances and locales in the brochure 'Venezia da vivere – La Guida', issued every three months or by calling Tel. 04 15 22 23 76).* Cinema aficionados will enjoy the summer ★ open-air-cinema in *Campo San Polo* (programme on posters and in the daily papers).

THEATRE

In the mid-16th century Venice saw the birth of that archetypal Italian theatre form, the commedia dell'arte. It's usually described as improvised and comical because only the rough scenario has been handed down for many beloved pieces and because – according to early sources – performances were so lively and characterisations so telling that audiences really thought the players were acting spontaneously. However, what was put on was written down somewhere. Moreover, pieces and performance followed strict rules. What began as frolics with local allusions and gossip grew into touring repertory theatre, ultimately going far afield – and strongly influencing such greats as Molière and Nestroy and, of course, the Viennese Volkstheater.

Again, it was Venice that shaped the course taken by the commedia dell'arte. Not confining their support to the visual arts and music, the Doges and the Council were ardent theatre-goers from the beginning. By 1637 the Cassiano Theatre, the world's first known opera house, was open for business, followed in 1678 by the Malibran and Goldoni Theatres, which put on plays. Venice has always loved the theatre and it's only fitting that Shakespeare, too, paid tribute to the city and its theatre.

Another fan of commedia dell' arte was that most voracious of German culture princes, the polymath Johann Wolfgang Goethe. He descended on it with his usual vigour: 'Yesterday I was at a comedy which gave me great pleasure: I saw an extemporaneous piece performed with masks with a deal of dash, energy and bravura.' It hasn't lost any of its bravura with the centuries. If the world-famous 'Goldoni' is putting on a Verdi opera or a Goldoni comedy and if you manage to find a ticket, clutch it in your fist and go! You really don't need to know Italian to enjoy yourself.

Avogaria **(100/A4)**
This little theatre puts on pieces in the melodic Venetian dialect. *Campo San Sebastiano, 1617, Tel. 04 15 20 61 30, landing-stage: San Basilio*

La Fenice **(102/A3)**
After the tragic fire – was it sabotage? – now just a memory. If you've never been inside it, shut your eyes and think of Guardi. An evening at this, one of the world's most famous opera houses, was a memorable event. And then on 29 January 1996 it was gutted by fire. Since then, Venice has had to make do with an outsized tent on Tronchetto called the Palafenice. By contrast, its portal opening on to the Campo San Fantin made the real Teatro look small although it seated 820. Rossini's 'Semiramis' (1823) and Verdi's 'La Traviata' (1853) had their premières here and leading singers and conductors loved La Fenice. But, as one expects of a 'fenice' – a 'phoenix' – or, mythically, a firebird, it will rise from the ashes in 2001. *Campo San Fantin, 2549, landing-stage: Giglio*

Goldoni **(102/B1)**
Here both musical events and modern theatre performances are staged. If a real Goldoni is on the programme, don't miss it. Tickets on sale at the box office: Mon–Sat 10 am–1 pm and 4.30 pm–7 am, evening box office just 30 minutes before the curtain goes up. Tickets start at L11,000. *Calle del Teatro, 4650, Tel. 04 15 20 54 22, 04 15 20 75 83, landing-stage: Rialto*

VENETIAN FOLK MUSIC

Ai Musicanti **(102/B2)**
Although audiences are international and, let's face it, touristy, this is one way of experiencing grass-roots Venetian culture. The Italian songs and folk-songs you'll here are real and performed all year round, twice an evening, at 7.30 pm and again at 9.30 pm, by Venetian artists. *Campo San Gallo, 1092, Tel. 04 15 20 89 22, landing-stage: San Marco*

Walks along canals and in alleys

These walking tours are marked in green on the map on the back cover and in the Street Atlas beginning on page 96

① THE REAL VENICE

You start out at Santa Lucia Station and go all the way to Dorsodouro through a maze of labyrinthine alleys and lovely squares, beautiful churches and scuole. Dorsoduro is probably the most unspoilt part of the city, the section of it where everyday life is going on. If you want to see some of the sights from inside and take a break or two for an espresso or a glass of prosecco, you'd better plan on at least half a day for this tour.

Start out where most visitors first set foot on Venetian pavement: in front of Santa Lucia Station, a dreary post-war building you'll want to turn your back on as fast as possible. Passing the *Chiesa degli Scalzi (p. 19)*, the church of the 'mendicant Carmelites', you cross over the bridge of the same name to the south bank of the Canal Grande. From here you follow the yellow signs for the 'Frari', which direct you southeast through a narrow alley and then along an equally narrow canal. After changing direction abruptly more than once, you'll be gazing up at one of the city's grandest churches: *Santa Maria Gloriosa dei Frari (p. 29)*. Its façade is austere, suitably so for a church built by a mendicant order of Franciscans. The unassuming façade conceals a treasure trove of great art. You can't miss Titian's 'Assumption' above the high altar, the aged painter's marble tomb and, diagonally across from it, the pyramidal funerary monument of the sculptor Antonio Canova. Spend some time admiring the magnificent choir loft, the Giovanni Bellini triptych (in the sacristy), the celebrated Titian Pesaro Madonna (right next to the side entrance), the Bartolomeo Vivarini altarpiece and pause at the tomb of the great early opera and madrigal composer, Claudio Monteverdi (both in the chancel chapels), whose career ended in Venice. To the south of the Frari is another great temple to art – the *Scuola Grande di San Rocco (p. 43)*. A Renaissance building, it was decorated throughout with paintings by Tintoretto. Like the Sistine Chapel, an unforgettable spatial experience!

Then you go back towards the Frari portal, turn right and cross a canal and you're at the church of *San Pantalon*, which boasts an enormous Baroque ceiling painting – go on past it to the *Campo di Santa Margherita*. This elongated rectangle is one of the most charming squares in Venice, entirely unspoilt and ready to assuage your hunger and thirst. It has a fish and a fruit market, a wine tavern, several bars and an excellent ice-cream parlour. The cube-shaped building at the centre was once the tanners' and dyers' guildhall. Art lovers will continue on to the southern tip of the Campo to visit the *Scuola Grande dei Carmini (p. 43)*, which has ceiling frescoes by Giambattista Tiepolo. You should include the pretty church associated with it in your visit.

Following the canal behind the Carmelite school, you pass the *Palazzo Zenobio* (Nr. 2596) on your left, an Armenian college since 1850 with a magnificent 18th-century ballroom and park. (Don't be afraid to ring the bell! Visitors are sometimes invited in to marvel at the spectacular 18th-century interior.) Continue on down the canal, turn left and cross the bridge to reach the *Campo Angelo Raffaele.* The church is only moderately interesting but the trattoria diagonally across from it and named after it serves superb seafood.

West of this last Campo is the residential section of *Santa Marta.* Here, down near the harbour, you'll see Venice at its most run-down and poor. Dilapidated tenements, a closed-down cotton mill and a sprinkling of factory ruins recall the industrial past of this quarter. The little church of *San Nicolò dei Mendicoli* brings a touch of the Middle Ages to what is otherwise depressingly real, post-industrial poverty.

If you go back across the Campo Angelo Raffaele and turn right, you'll soon come to the recently and superbly restored church of *San Sebastiano (p. 28)*. In it are a magnificent cycle of paintings by Paolo Veronese and the painter's tomb. Two minutes' walk from there suddenly takes you out into the open on the broad Canale della Giudecca and you're overwhelmed by Guardi. On the horizon you'll see the La Giudecca skyline, the massive Stucky mill and the dome of the Redentore.

You aren't footsore and weary? If not, turn left and stroll down the broad pavement called the *Záttere.* Now you're back with the crisp clarity of Canaletto. Stay on the Záttere for one and a half km to the *Dogana,* the Customs building at the eastern tip of Dorsoduro, where you have a breathtaking panorama of the Doge's Palace, the Campanile and the monastery of San Giorgio Maggiore. Bars and restaurants tempt you along the way.

② VENICE AHOY: BY BOAT ROUND THE OLD CITY

The best way of discovering the historic core of the city is by taking to the water. Our tip: instead of the classic trip down the main traffic artery, the Canal Grande, go round Venice by water and see the pearl of the lagoon from the outside. On board a no. 42 vaporetto you'll see the Cannaregio district, which is not so familiar to visitors, and the harbour district. You'll have panoramic views of the finest promenades. Departure: Santa Lucia Station or Piazzale Roma. Time frame: including 'excursions ashore' a whole day.

Again you start off at Santa Lucia Station. However, this time you take a water-bus right at the foot of the stairs, a no. 42 vaporetto. It putters down the Canal Grande for a while but soon – right after the grand church of San Geremia – it turns left into the Canale di Cannaregio. Passing the *Palazzo Labia (p. 19)*, which houses the Italian state-owned radio and TV conglomerate RAI, your vaporetto heads straight into the Cannaregio district, which is remarkably spacious and open by Venetian standards. We recommend you take advantage of the very first stop *(Ponte delle Guglie, p. 17)* to go ashore and visit the former Jewish *ghetto (p. 32)*, Europe's oldest, and the one that made the term generic, whatever the derivation of the word (Venetian geto for foundry or the shortened diminutive of Italian borgetto, little borough). Here you can go to the excellent *Hebrew Museum (p. 39)* and visit several historic synagogues, two of which are still used daily, one in winter and the other in summer.

Once you've caught the waterbus again, your route continues on under the *Ponte dei Tre Archi*, the only three-arched bridge in Venice, and out into open water. From here you can see across the northern lagoon as far as Burano, Torcello and the airport on the mainland. The vaporetto heads east, passing the northern section of the old city bristling with church towers. Your next venture ashore should be at the *Madonna dell'Orto* landing-stage, where you can see the lovely Gothic *church (p. 28)* of that name and the house where *Jacopo Tintoretto died (p. 28)*, near the church. The next stop, *Fondamenta Nuove*, is again a good place to go ashore. Here you'll see the Baroque Jesuit church of *Santa Maria Assunta dei Gesuiti* and, very close by is *Titian's house*, so go see that too.

Now the vaporetto putters across to *San Michele (p. 23)*, the island of the dead. The northernmost stop on this trip is at the glass-blowing island of *Murano (p. 25)*. Art lovers will not let souvenir hunters deter them from a visit to the churches of *San Pietro Martire* and *Santi Maria e Donato*, next to the glass museum. If you're dying to see the *glass-blowing industry*, this is where it is.

Back across the water, the vaporetto follows the Fondamenta Nuove along the north shore of the Castello district of Venice, past the Franciscan church of San Francesco della Vigna and goes around the *San Pietro di Castello and Isola di Sant'Elena Peninsulas*. In the Basin of San Marco it continues on past the green space that is the Giardini Pubblici and the site of the Biennale. Several countries have distinctive permanent pavilions there. At the *Museo Storico Navale (p. 41)* it reaches the Basin of San Marco and heads westward. Along the *Riva degli Schiavoni*, the pavement built by the Dalmatians and popular with walkers because it's so wide, many of the city's most famous luxury hotels pass in review: the Danieli, Gabrielli Sandwirth, Londra Palace, Metropole and so on. Once you've arrived at the *San Zaccaria* landing-stage and feel you've really got your sea legs now (and vaporetto travel in Venice is dangerously addictive), you can keep on the no. 51 line across to the *Lido (p. 29)* and return from there along La Giudecca to the Piazzale Roma with the no. 52 line.

③ IN PALLADIO'S FOOTSTEPS

A walk to the magnificent ecclesiastical architecture for which the great architect from Padua was famous. You should allow at least two and preferably three hours for going to the two southern islands of San Giorgio Maggiore and La Giudecca.

A veduta from the modern standpoint, one of the most frequently photographed views: the monastery of *San Giorgio Maggiore (p. 28)*, which Andrea Palladio built in the mid-16th century for the Benedictines on the lovely island across from the Doge's Palace. You take the no. 82 vaporetto from the San Zaccaria landing-stage to cross over in just a few minutes. On arrival, take some time just to gaze in wonder at the brilliant white marble façade, which, in its austere geometry, is so reminiscent of an ancient temple, before going into the church. No less awe-inspiring than its façade, the church nave has three aisles and is decorated with huge Tintoretto frescoes. Unfortunately, the famous monastery refectory, the library and the staircase are all off bounds for tourists. As a consolation prize, you are permitted to ascend the *campanile* and the panoramic view from its observation platform is every bit as breathtaking as the one you have from the San Marco campanile across the water.

All you have to do if you want to admire another Palladian masterpiece is stick with the same water-bus line for two more stops. The church of *Il Redentore (p. 28)* was built on the neighbouring island of La Giudecca in thanksgiving for deliverance from a plague. Commissioned by the Republican government and consecrated in 1592, it exemplifies Palladian architecture with its impressive dome and marble façade. Every year on the third Sunday in July it is the focal point of a major festival with fireworks and all night picnics on the water.

Only a few minutes' walk to the east, still along the north pavement of La Giudecca, takes you to the church of *Santa Maria della Presentazione.* This one is also attributed to Andrea Palladio, albeit erroneously. It doesn't always have to be Palladio, whose work was certainly not always as austerely simple as this. For a treat, it is inviting to take some time to visit the small church which is also known as Le Zitelle, even though it doesn't belong to the given topic. Its harmonic proportions make it impressive in itself *(unfortunately, it's only open Sun 10 am–11.30 am).*

A postscript on Palladianism: If you want to go on studying the work of Europe's first professional architect in Venice, go to the northern part of the Castello district next. There, not far from the western Arsenal wall is the church of *San Francesco della Vigna.* Built in the 1560s, this one exemplifies Palladio's eager response to classical antiquity. Architectural historians regard its façade as a milestone in the development of Classicism before Palladio turned to Mannerism.

Practical information

Important addresses and useful information for your visit to Venice

AMERICAN & BRITISH ENGLISH

Marco Polo travel guides are written in British English. In North America, certain terms and usages deviate from British usage. Some of the more frequently encountered examples are:
baggage for luggage, billion for milliard, cab for taxi, car rental for car hire, drugstore for chemist's, fall for autumn, first floor for groundfloor, freeway/highway for motorway, gas(oline) for petrol, railroad for railway, restroom for toilet/lavatory, streetcar for tram, subway for underground/tube, toll-free numbers for freephone numbers, trailer for caravan, trunk for boot, vacation for holiday, wait staff for waiting staff (in restaurants etc.), zip code for postal code.

BOAT RENTAL

You can rent a boat from the following *Gianpietro Brussa* in *Cannaregio (Tel. 041 71 57 87)* and from *Luigi Seno* in *Dorsoduro (Tel. 04 15 23 13 00)*. For motorboat rental see *Oscar Secco* in *Castello (Tel. 04 15 23 10 54)*.

CAR RENTAL

For trips on the mainland the best thing to do is rent a car at *Piazzale Roma* in Venice or in *Mestre* on the mainland. You'll have to pay approx L150,000 to 180,000 a day for a small car.

CLOTHING

Since the 1990s there have been fines (up to L30,000) for visitors who appear topless or in beachwear in the city of Venice.

COMPLAINTS

Call the toll-free 'complaints number' Venezia No Problem *800 35 59 20* if you want to take up the Venice tourist asssociation's remarkable offer of allowing visitors to the city to register complaints round the clock about public services or behaviour which is in some way unpleasant, harrassing or discriminatory to tourists visiting the city.

CONSULATES & EMBASSIES

British Consulate
Accademia Dorsoduro 1051, 30123 Venezia, Tel. 041 522 72 07

Canadian Consulate
Via Zara 30, 00198 Rome Tel. 06 445 98 11

Embassy of the United States
Via Vittorio Veneto 119a, 00187 Rome, Tel. 06 467 41

CULTURAL INFORMATION

The best place for finding out all the current cultural events and opening hours and keep up on what is happening in Venice is the daily paper 'Il Gazzettino' and two bilingual (Italian/English) brochures 'Un Ospite di Venezia' (monthly) and 'Venice pocket' (four times a year). The two brochures are available at all information centres, hotel desks, travel agents, etc.

CURRENCY

Banks and savings and loan institutions have uniform opening hours in Venice: *Mon–Fri 8.30 am–1.30 pm and 2.35 pm–3.35 pm.* Euro-cheques are cashed up to a value of L300,000. To cash them, you'll probably have to show your passport. There is an exchange bureau at Santa Lucia Station, *daily 8 am–8 pm.* It's simpler to use the ubiquitous cashpoints (US English: ATMs). The standard international credit cards are accepted at nearly all hotels, most restaurants and many shops.

CUSTOMS

Within the EU tourists possessing anything needed for personal use is duty-free, e. g. 90 l wine, 10 l spirits over 40 %, 800 cigarettes, 400 cigarillos. Remember, customs restrictions for travellers returning to Canada, the US and the UK prohibit the import of cured or raw meat, fresh fruits, vegetables, cheeses and bread, etc.

DISABLED PERSONS

Its innumerable bridges make getting about in Venice difficult indeed for disabled persons. However, embarking and disembarking from *vaporetti* is relatively easy because everything is on the same level. There are toilet facilities for disabled persons at the following locations: Piazzale Roma, at the Stazione Marittima, on both sides of the Rialto Bridge, in the Doge's Palace, on the Biennale grounds and on the Campo San Luca.

DOGS

Dogs (visitors' dogs too) must be muzzled at all times in the street. You must buy a regular ticket for an adult if you take a dog on water-buses.

EMERGENCIES

Carabinieri *112;* ambulance *113;* fire *115;* hospital Ospedale Civile *04 15 29 45 17*

GONDOLAS

There are eleven different landing-stages along the Canal Grande where you can step into a gondola. The official rate is L120,000 for 50 minutes (between 8 pm and 8 am: a surcharge of L30,000). There's room for up to six people in a gondola. If the above prices seem too steep for you, you can still have the thrill of a ride in one. Gondola ferries, which take passengers across the Canal Grande for L1,000 (one way) depart from landing-stages at Santa Lucia Station, at San Marcuola, at Santa Sofia next to the Ca' d'Oro, at the Riva del Carbon next to the Rialto Bridge, at San Tomà, between San Samuele and Ca' Rezzonico as well as at Santa

Maria del Giglio. From May to September there are evening gondola trips with music.

GUIDED TOURS

You can book an official tour guide through the *Cooperativa Guide Turistiche (San Marco, 750 (near San Zulian), Tel. 04 15 20 90 38, Fax 04 15 21 07 62).* Book well in advance! Special theme tours take place on a regular basis, including: 'Secret Itinerary through the Doge's Palace' *(Gli itinerari segreti), daily 10 am and noon, only in Italian, L24,000 per person, booking Tel. 04 15 22 49 51;* 'In Richard Wagner's Foot-steps' through the Palazzo Vendramin-Calergi, *every Sat morning, English, information and booking Tel. (Fri mornings) 04 15 23 25 44;* 'The History of Venetian Music', *on the 1st Sat of every month, information and booking Tel. 04 15 23 06 16;* 'Venus in Venice: Love Trysts', *Fri 5 pm, information and booking Tel. 041 63 07 61;* 'In the Footsteps of Sherlock Holmes', *Sun 11 am (Italian, French, English), meet at: landing-stage San Stae, Info-Tel. 04 15 23 07 49*

HIGH WATER

During the autumn and winter months the threat of *acqua alta* is always with you. If a flood is imminent, a siren alert sounds to warn everyone. For natives of the city the sound means pulling on their boots and even waders. Visitors are advised to seek out places that are at least 50 cm above pavement level and while away the time until the all-clear sounds, usually after only a few hours. At certain *vaporetto* landing-stages plans are hung out on which the boardwalks are drawn in enabling you to reach most destinations in the city without wet feet.

INFORMATION

Ente Nazionale Italiano per il Turismo – ENIT (Italian state tourist office)

In the UK:
1 Princes Street, London W1R 8AY; Tel. 0171/408 12 54

In the USA:
Suite 1565, 630 Fifth Avenue, New York, NY 10111; Tel. 212/245 56 18

In Canada:
Suite 1914, 1 Place de Ville Marie, Montréal, Québec H3B 2C3, Tel. 514/866 76 67

INFORMATION IN VENICE

Azienda di Promozione Turistica
The Italian state tourist office has five offices here *(uffici informazioni):* at *Santa Lucia Train Station* and at *the airport (both all year round, daily 9.30 am–6.30 pm),* on the *Lido (Viale Santa Maria Elisabetta, 6a)* and in *Ca' Savio (Via Fausta, 70, both mid-May till end Sep daily 9.30 am–12.30 and 6 pm–8 pm).* A travel centre in the *Palazzetto della Selva at the San Marco landing-stage* has recently been reopened *(daily 9 am–7.30 pm).* To contact the head tourist information office call: *Tel. 04 15 29 87 11, Fax 04 1523 03 99, I-30122 Venezia, Castello, 4421, www.provincia.venezia.it*

LANGUAGE COURSES

If you want to learn Italian in Venice, the following institutes offer courses taught by trained language teachers: *Società Dante Alighieri, Ponte del Purgatorio (next to the Arsenal Portal) in Castello, Tel. 04 15 28 91 27; Istituto Zambler, Campo Santa Margherita, 3116a, Tel. 04 15 22 43 31, e-mail: zambler@tin.it.; Centro Linguistico Interfacoltà, Calle Bonvicini, 2161, Tel. 04 15 20 36 69; Centro Culturale Italiano per Stranieri 'Serenissima', Calle Lunga Santa Maria Formosa, 5170, Tel. 04 15 22 91 13*

LOST PROPERTY (UFFICI OGGETTI RINVENUTI)

The two official lost & found offices are at Santa Lucia Station: (**96/A3-4**) *daily 8 am–noon and 3 pm–6 pm, Tel. 041 78 52 38, landing-stage: Ferrovia,* and in the city police office in the Town Hall: (**102/A1**) *Palazzo Loredan, Riva del Carbon, daily 8 am–noon and 3 pm–6 pm, Tel. 04 15 22 40 63 or 04 15 23 60 10, landing-stage: Rialto*

MEASURES & WEIGHTS

1 cm	0.39 inches
1 m	1.09 yards (3.28 feet)
1 km	0.62 miles
1 m²	1.20 sq. yards
1 ha	2.47 acres
1 km²	0.39 sq. miles
1 g	0.035 ounces
1 kg	2.21 pounds
1 British tonne	*1016 kg*
1 US ton	*907 kg*

1 litre is equivalent to 0.22 Imperial gallons and 0.26 US gallons

MOSQUITOES

Mosquitoes can be a real nuisance, especially on the islands in summer. You're advised to take insect repellent with you.

PHARMACIES (FARMACIE)

Mon–Fri 9 am–12.30 and 4 pm–7.45 pm in summer, 3.30 pm–7.15 pm in winter, Sat only mornings. Lists of open pharmacies are posted on every pharmacy. *Telephone information: 192*

PORTERS

These strong and willing helpers are often needed in this carless city with all those bridges and alleys. You can engage their services at the following locations: Santa Lucia Station, Piazzale Roma, Accademia, Rialto, San Geremia, San Marco/clock tower, San Marco/Bacino Orseolo, Calle Vallaresso. Prices are set and regulated by the city authorities. Within the old city, one piece of luggage costs L20,000 (to the Lido, La Giudecca or to other islands L40,000), two pieces of luggage: L30,000 (50,000), three or four pieces: L40,000 (70,000), each piece beyond four: L10,000 (15,000). For a distance of less than 50 m porter service costs L1,500, to 300 m L2,000 per piece of luggage.

POST & TELEPHONE

The main post office (**98/B5**) is in what was once the Fondaco dei Tedeschi. Hours of business: Mon–Sat 8.30 am–6 pm. Stamps *(francobolli)* and telephone cards are also available at tobacconists. You'll spot the latter by a sign with a white T on a black background.
The best way of placing local and long-distance calls is to use public telephone call-boxes. To use these you need a phone card which you can obtain at any tobacconist's and at many bank branches for

L10,000, 20,000 or 50,000. To call abroad from Venice, dial 00 1 for the US and Canada, 00 44 for the UK and 00 353 for the Republic of Ireland. To call Italy from abroad, dial 00 39, then the number including the first 0: what was formerly the dialling code (area code) for Venice 041 is now integrated in Venice number you are calling.

PUBLIC TOILETS

Day-trippers and indeed all visitors feel reassured on hearing that public toilets are available. The availability of public toilet facilities is particularly important in Venice because many bars and small eateries still do not have toilets. Clean public toilets, which of course are not free of charge, are available in both *alberghi diurni* (day hotels in which you can also take showers) at Santa Lucia Station, *daily 6 am–8.30 pm,* and next to the post office on the west side of St Mark's Square, *daily 8.30 am–8 pm.* There is also a public WC on the Campo San Bartolomeo. In addition, all museums have public toilets.

STUDY IN VENICE

For a six-months' to one-year course of study in Venice (American-run), contact *Tae Gladys Krieble, Delmas Foundation* **(101/E1)**, *521 Fifth Avenue, Suite 1612 New York, 10175-1699 NewYork, USA Tel. 212 68 70 01 1, Fax 212 687 88 77*

TAXIS

Since the main traffic arteries in Venice are the canals between the various islands and small islands, the city's taxi service consists of motorboats *(motoscafi),* or water taxis. Not all water taxis have been equipped with meters. Nevertheless, the drivers must keep to the established rates, which are supposed to be posted in their boats where passengers can see them. The flat-rate fares are for four people. There is a surcharge for night service and service on national holidays as well as for luggage and waiting time. Landing-stages are at the following: *Santa Lucia Station,* at *Piazzale Roma,* at the *Molo San Marco,* at the *Ponte di Rialto,* on the island of *Tronchetto,* on the *Lido* und at the *airport.* Between San Marco and the airport a semi-public water taxi service operates for *L17,000, Tel. 04 15 23 57 75).*

THEATRE TICKETS

Most hotels will be glad to help you with booking theatre tickets. Perhaps the simplest way of going about it is to ask a travel agent. The following often have tickets:
CIT: **(102/C3)** *Piazza San Marco, 48/50, Tel. 04 15 28 54 80 Waggons-Lit/Cook:* **(103/D2)** *Piazzetta dei Leoni, 289-305, Tel. 04 15 22 34 05*
American Express: **(102/B3)** *Salizzada San Moisè, 1471, Tel. 04 15 20 08 44*
Bassani: **(102/B3)** *Via Larga XXII Marzo, 2414, Tel. 04 15 20 86 33*

TIPPING

A service charge is usually included in restaurant prices. However, waiters, chambermaids and gondolieri of course like to know that the friendly service they offer is appreciated. In restaurants it's a good idea to stick to the standard rate: five to ten per cent of the bill. When you pay, please don't tell the waiter to deduct for a tip. You leave your tip on the plate your bill was on or on the table when you leave the restaurant. In hotels you give the bellboy who has carried up your bags up to L2,500. In bars you leave a tip after *caffè* and *panino* on the counter, ranging between L100 and L200. Gondoliers receive tips ranging between L2,000 and L5,000. You simply round off the bill for a water taxi.

WATER-BUS SERVICE

The public transport system consists of 19 water-bus (vaporetto/i) lines. Some only run in summer. The fare is a uniform L6,000 Lit for a single (one-way) ticket to all destinations. There are fare reductions, for instance the *biglietto 24 ore*, with which you can go for L18,000 on all routes. The practical three-day ticket for weekend trippers costs L35,000. For information ask at the *Azienda del Consorzio Trasporti Veneziano* (ACTV) at Piazzale Roma (**96/A5**), *daily 7.30 am–8 pm, Tel. 04 15 28 78 86.*

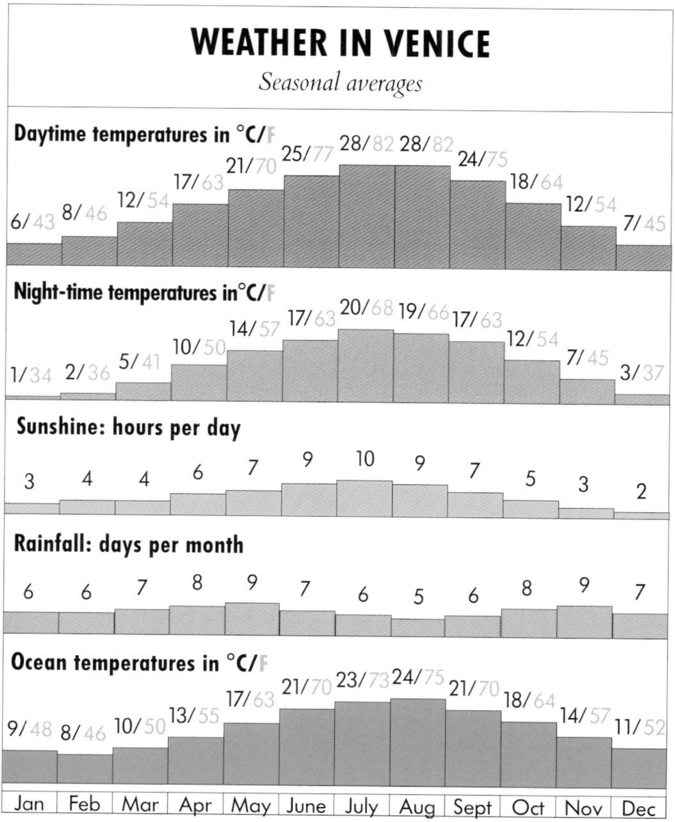

Do's and don'ts

A few pointers on how not to spoil your trip to Venice

Don't disrupt divine service
You might well happen to be visiting a church while divine service is going on. Mass is held daily (!) in St Mark's Cathedral alone from 7 am throughout the morning every 45 minutes. However, mass in St Mark's is confined to a closed-off side aisle. In any case, you shouldn't disturb worshippers by taking flash pictures, talking or laughing. Remember to be suitably dressed whenever you're visiting churches.

Don't buy masks
You'll probably soon be fed up when all the souvenir shops and kiosks round St Mark's Square try to sell you a Carnival mask as well as postcards and other staples you might expect to find there. The masks sold at souvenir shops are mass-produced and range from lapel-pin size to elephant size. There are a few places where you can buy hand-made masks but certainly not at souvenir shops.

Don't waste time in Mestre
If you haven't all that much time, don't waste what you do have by going over to Mestre on the mainland. Mestre is the residential section of an industrial suburb and has mushroomed with urban sprawl. The population of Mestre has rapidly grown to over 220,000.

Don't waste money in Murano
Since we're already on the subject of wasting: you don't have to spend any money in Murano. There are still some glass-blowers there but most of what is produced for sale is horrendous kitsch. The Museo Vetrario does, however, exhibit some magnificent pieces. Admire those and leave the breakable souvenirs in the shops.

Don't feed the pigeons
Pedlars hawk little bags of corn for feeding the flocks of pigeons. These pests are fat enough anyway (and carry respiratory diseases like psittacosis). If you do feel sorry for the pedlars or the pigeons and buy some pigeon feed, don't throw away the plastic bag. A city ordinance posted on the stall where you bought it warns you you'll pay a heavy fine for littering if you do leave bags about.

Don't arrive without sweaters
Venice is damp and don't let anyone tell you otherwise. Evenings are cool and you'll always be glad to have a warm sweater, even in summer. At some times of the year you'll reach for boots and a raincoat, too.

Street Atlas of Venice

Please refer to back cover for an overview of this Street Atlas

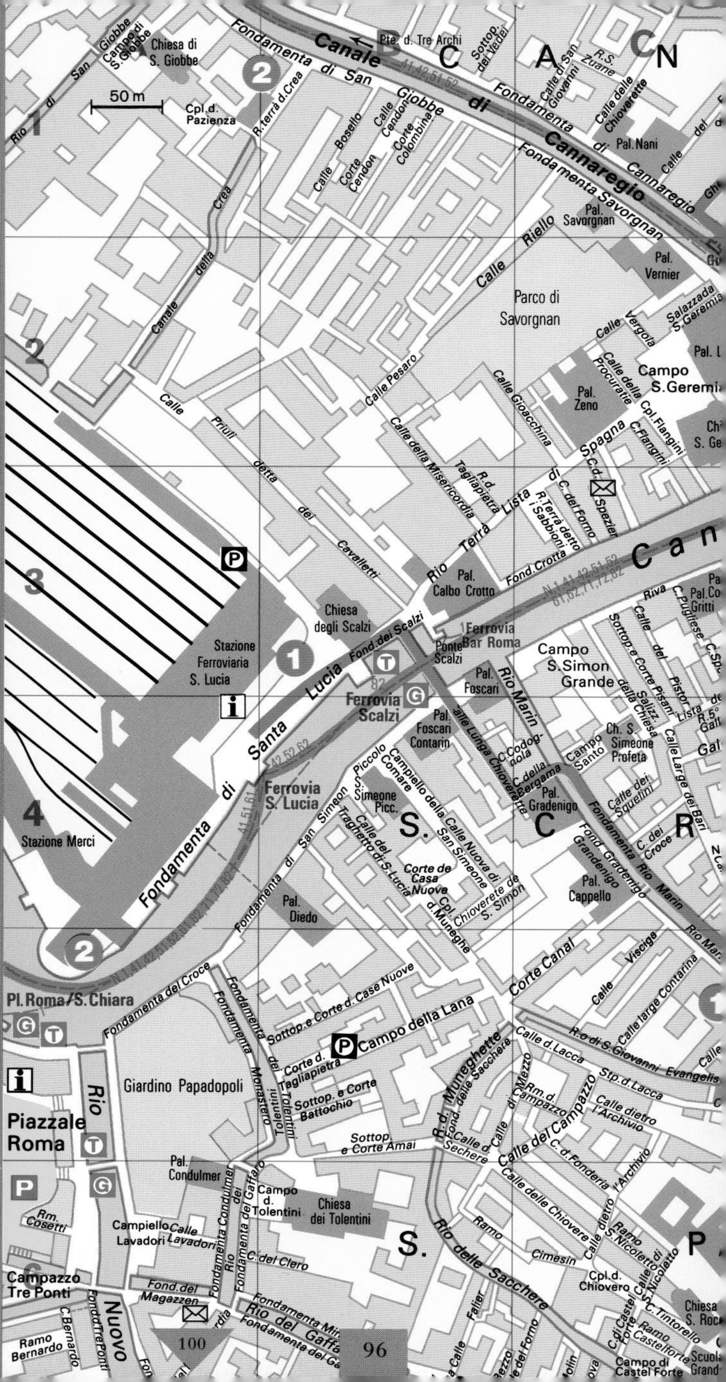

Canale di Cannaregio
Fondamenta di San Giobbe
Fondamenta di Cannaregio
Fondamenta Savorgnan
Pte. d. Tre Archi
Chiesa di S. Giobbe
Campo di S. Giobbe
Rio di San Giobbe
50 m
Cpl.d. Pazienza
R.terrà d.Crea
Canale della Crea
Calle Bosello
Corte Cendon
Calle Cendon
Corte Colombina
Sottop. dei Vedei
Calle di San Giovanni
R.S. Zuane
Calle delle Chiovarette
Pal. Nani
Pal. Savorgnan
Pal. Vernier
Calle Riello
Parco di Savorgnan
Calle Vergola
Salazzada S.Geremia
Calle della Procuratie
Campo S.Geremia
Pal. Zeno
Calle Gioacchina
Cpl.Flangini
C.Flangini
Spagna
C.d. Spezier
Calle Pesaro
Calle Priuli detta dei Cavalletti
Calle della Misericordia
R.d. Tagliapietra
Rio Terrà Lista di Spagna
R.Terrà detto i Sabbioni
C. del Forno
Fond.Crotta
Pal. Calbo Crotto
Canal
Riva
Pal. Gritti
C.Pugliese
Chiesa degli Scalzi
Stazione Ferroviaria S. Lucia
Stazione Merci
Fond.dei Scalzi
Fondamenta di Santa Lucia
Ferrovia Bar Roma
Ponte Scalzi
Ferrovia Scalzi
Ferrovia S. Lucia
Campo S.Simon Grande
Pal. Foscari
Rio Marin
Pal. Foscari Contarin
Calle Lunga Chioverette
C.Codognola
C.della Bergama
Campo Santo
Ch. S. Simeone Profeta
Sottop.e Corte Pisani
Salizz. della Chiesa
Calle del Pistor
Lista de
Calle Large dei Bari
Calle dei Squelini
Pal. Gradenigo
Fondamenta Rio Marin
Fond. Gradenigo
C. dei Croce
Piccolo S. Simeone
Comare
Campiello della Comare
S. Simeone Picc.
Calle Nuova di San Simeone
Calle del Traghetto di S.Lucia
Fondamenta di San Simeon
Corte de Casa Nuove
Cpl. d.Muneghe
Chioverete de S. Simon
Pal. Diedo
Pal. Cappello
Corte Canal
Calle Visiga
Calle large Contarina
R.o di S.Giovanni Evangelista
Calle d.Lacca
Stp.d.Lacca
Pl.Roma/S.Chiara
Fondamenta del Croce
Fondamenta Minotto
Fondamenta dei Tolentini
Sottop.e Corte d. Case Nuove
Campo della Lana
Corte d. Tagliapietra
Sottop. e Corte Battochio
Sottop. e Corte Amai
R.d. Muneghette
Fond. delle Sacchere
Calle del Campazzo
Rm.d. Campazzo
Calle dietro l'Archivio
C.d.Fonderia
Calle delle Chiovere
Giardino Papadopoli
Piazzale Roma
Rio Nuovo
Pal. Condulmer
Campo d. Tolentini
Chiesa dei Tolentini
Fondamenta Condulmer
Fondamenta del Gaffaro
Rio del Gaffaro
C.del Clero
Campiello Lavadori
Calle Lavadori
Rm. Cosetti
Campazzo Tre Ponti
Fond.del Magazzen
Fond.d.TrePonti
C.Bernardo
Ramo Bernardo
Rio delle Sacchere
Ramo Cimesin
Cpl.d. Chiovero
Calle dietro S.Nicoletto
Calle di S.Nicoletto
C.Tintorello
Chiesa S. Rocco
Ramo Castelforte
C.di Castel Forte
Campo di Castel Forte
Scuola Grande
S. Croce
S. P
100

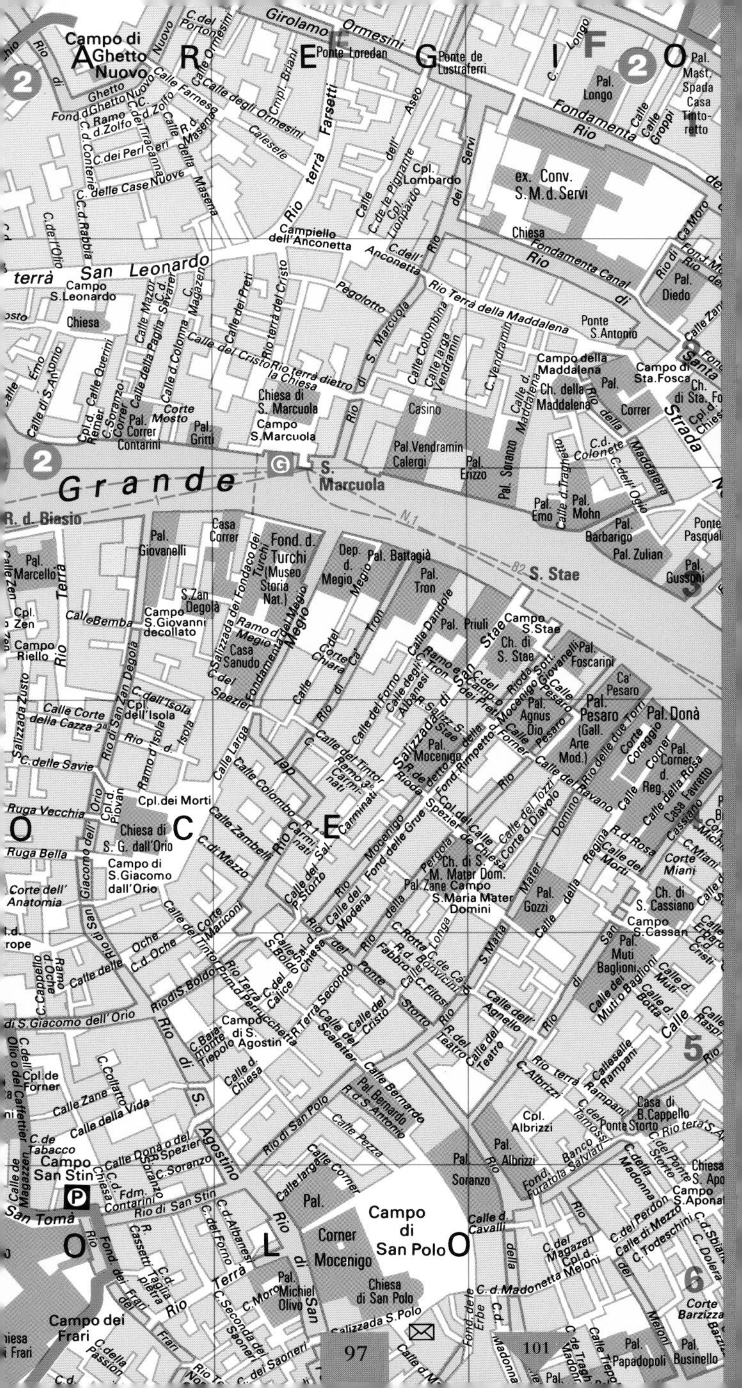

Campo di Ghetto Nuovo
Ghetto Nuovo
Fond. d. Ghetto Nuovo
Calle Farnese
Calle degli Ormesini
Girolamo Ormesini
Ponte Loredan
Ponte de Lustraferri
Cmpl. Briani
Rio terrà Farsetti
Caleselle
Calle dell' Aseo
Cpl. Lombardo
Calle de la Pignate
Cpl. Lionpardo
Rio dei Servi
Pal. Longo
Fondamenta Rio
Calle Groppi
Pal. Mast. Spada
Casa Tintoretto
ex. Conv. S.M.d. Servi
Chiesa
Fondamenta Canal
Rio di Ca Moro
Pal. Diedo
C. delle Case Nuove
C. d. Rabbia
C. dei Perl
Calle della Masena
Campiello dell'Anconetta
C. dell' Anconetta
Pegolotto
Rio Terrà della Maddalena
terrà San Leonardo
Campo S. Leonardo
Chiesa
Calle Mazor
C. d. Savarer
C. Magazen
Calle dei Preti
Rio terrà del Cristo
Calle del Cristo
Rio terrà dietro la Chiesa
Calle della Paglia
Calle d. Colonna
Calle Querini
Calle di S. Antonio
Emo
Cpl. d. Remer
C. Soranzo Correr
Pal. Correr Contarini
Corte Mosto
Pal. Gritti
Chiesa di S. Marcuola
Campo S. Marcuola
Rio di S. Marcuola
Calle Colombina
Calle larga Vendramin
C. Vendramin
Casino
Pal. Vendramin Calergi
Pal. Erizzo
Pal. Soranzo
Calle d. Maddalena
Campo della Maddalena
Ch. della Maddalena
Rio della Maddalena
Pal. Correr
Campo di Sta. Fosca
Ch. di Sta. Fosca
Strada
Ponte S. Antonio
C. d. Colonete
C. dell' Ogio
Calle d. Traghetto
Pal. Emo
Pal. Mohn
Pal. Barbarigo
Pal. Zulian
Pal. Gussoni
Ponte Pasquali
Grande
S. Marcuola
N. 1
82
S. Stae
R. d. Biasio
Pal. Marcello
Rio Terrà
Pal. Giovanelli
Casa Correr
Fond. d. Turchi (Museo Storia Nat.)
Salizzada dei Fondaco dei Turchi
Dep. d. Megio
Pal. Battagià
Pal. Tron
Calle Dandolo
Pal. Priuli
Campo S. Stae
Ch. di S. Stae
Pal. Foscarini
Ca' Pesaro
Pal. Pesaro (Gall. Arte Mod.)
Pal. Donà
Cpl. Zen
Calle Bemba
Campo Riello
Campo S. Giovanni decollato
S. Zan Degolà
Ramo d. Megio
Fondamenta del Megio
Casa Sanudo
C. del Spezier
Corte del Chiara
Calle Tron
Calle del Forno
Calle degli Albanesi
Salizzada di San Stae
Pal. Agnus Dio
Calle Pesaro
Rio delle due Torri
Corte Coreggio
Pal. Corner d. Reg.
Calle della Rosa
Casa Favretto
Salizzada Zusto
Calle Corte della Cazza 2a
Rio di San Zan Degolà
C. dell'Isola
Cpl. dell'Isola
Ramo d'Isola
Calle Larga
C. delle Savie
Calle del Tintor
Calle Colombo
Pal. Mocenigo
Fond. Rimpetto Mocenigo
Calle del Ravano
Ruga Vecchia
Cpl. d. Piovan
Cpl. dei Morti
Chiesa di S. G. dall'Orio
Campo di S. Giacomo dall'Orio
Calle Zambelli
C. di Mezzo
Ruga Bella
Corte dell' Anatomia
Rio di San Giacomo dell' Orio
Rio Carminati
Fond. delle Grue
Calle della Pergola
Ch. di S. M. Mater Dom.
Pal. Zane Campo S. Maria Mater Domini
Calle del Tozzi
Corte d. Diavolo
Rio di Mater Domini
Pal. Gozzi
Calle della Regina
R. d. Rosa
Calle dei Morti
Corte Miani
Ch. di S. Cassiano
Campo S. Cassan
Calle Corte Mariconi
Calle del Tintor
Calle delle Oche
C. d. Oche
Ramo d. Oche
C. Cappello
Rio di S. Boldo
Rio Terrà Primo d. Perucchetta
Calle del Modena
Rio del Ponte Storto
Calle Longa
Rio di San Cassiano
Pal. Muti Baglioni
Calle dei Muti o Baglioni
Calle d. Botta
Calle d. Agnello
Rio terrà Secondo
Calle del Calice
Calle del Cristo
Campo di S. Agostin
C. Bajamonte Tiepolo
Calle d. Chiesa
Calle del Scaletter
Calle Bernardo
Pal. Bernardo
R. d. S. Antonio
Rio del Teatro
Calle del Teatro
C. Albrizzi
Rio terrà Rampani
Calleselle Rampani
Casa di B. Cappello
Ponte Storto
Rio di S. Agostin
Cpl. de Forner
C. Coltatto
Calle Zane
Calle della Vida
C. dell'Olio o del Caffettier
Campo San Stin
C. de Tabacco
Calle Donà o del Spezier
C. Soranzo
Fdm. Contarini
Rio di San Stin
Rio di San Polo
Calle Pezza
Calle larga Corner
Pal. Corner Mocenigo
Campo di San Polo
Pal. Soranzo
Pal. Albrizzi
Cpl. Albrizzi
Banco Salviati
Fond. Furatola
Calle d. Madonna
Calle del Ponte Storto
Chiesa S. Apo
Campo S. Aponal
C. del Perdon
Calle di Mezzo
C. Todeschini
San Tomà
Rio Terrà
Fond. dei Frari
R. Cassetti
C. d. Tagliapietra
C. del Forno
C. d. Albanesi
C. Seconda del Saoneri
C. Moro
Pal. Michiel Olivo
Chiesa di San Polo
Calle d. Cavalli
C. d. Madonetta
Cpl. d. Meloni
C. del Magazen
Rio dei Meloni
Campo dei Frari
Chiesa Frari
Calle della Passion
Salizzada S. Polo
Fond. de le Erbe
Pal. Papadopoli
Pal. Businello
Corte Barzizza
97
101

Sacca della Misericordia
Madonna dell' Orto
Zaffo
Ponte di Sacca
Pal. Mast. Spada
Casa Tintoretto
Calle Tintoretto
C.d.due Corti
Ramo dei Muti
Corte dei Muti
Rio dei Muti
Ponte Muti
Corte Vecchia
Fond. dell'Abbazia
Corte Nuova
C.d. Pignate
C.d. Zoccolo
C. Trevisan
Cpl.d. Trevisan
Rio della Sensa
Sottop. dell' Abbazia
Chiesa di S. M. Valverde
Campo d. Abbazia
Fond. dell'Abbazia
Canale della Misericordia
Ch. di S. Marziale
Campo S. Marziale
Rio della Misericordia
Calle Larga Lezze
Pal. Lezzo
Fond. della Misericordia
Calle Zancani
Rio del Trapolin
Fond. del Trapolin
Pal. Vendramin
Ch. Sta. Fosca
Cpl.d. Chiesa
Rio Santa Fosca
Pal. Giovanelli
Rio di Noale
Pal. Molin
Pal. Papafava
Calle Racchetta
Rio della Racchetta
Chiesa di S. Caterina
Fond. S. Caterina
Calle Boldù
S. Caterina
Calle d. Masena
Calle lunga
Fondamenta
Calle Marco Foscarini
Calle d. Consorti
Calle d. Legname
C.d. Scuola d. Botteri
C.d. Crociferi
R.d. Crociferi
Orat. d. Crociferi
Corte d. Candele
C.d. Candele
Cpl. S. Antonio
Pal. Zen
Fondamenta Zen
Rio di Santa Caterina
Campo d. Gesuiti
Ramo Squ. Vecchio
Rio della Racchetta
Fond. S. Andrea
di S. Andrea
Calle Zanardi
R. Zanardi
Rio di Ca' Dolce
C.d. Sartori
Fond. d. Sartori
Salizzada Seriman
Pal. Seriman
Fondamenta di San Felice
C. Salomon
R. dei Fiori
C.d. Stua
F. Stua
Rio di San Felice
Calle Priuli
Calle del Forno
C. delle Erbe
Calle Corrente
C. degli Albanesi
Ramo d. Albanesi
Rio della Guerra
Ruga due Pozzi
Fond. Priuli
Rio Priuli
Ponte Pasqualigo
Ch. di S. Felice
Campo S. Felice
Pal. Baldù
C.d. Traghetto
Ponte S. Felice
Cpl.d. Testori
C.d. Pistor
Calle Zotti
Calle delle Vele
Cpl. Priuli
C.d. Cristo
Corte d. Cristo
Calle del Forno
Rio terrà di Barba Fruttarol
C. Barbaro
Tagliapietra
Rio terrà d. Franceschi
C.d. Squero
C.d. Padiglion
Salizzada Borgato
C.d. Remer
C.d. Forno
C.d. Posta
Strada Nova
Pal. Fontana
Pal. Giusti
Ca' d'Oro
C.d. Ca' D'Oro
Pal. Pesaro
Pal. Sagredo
Ch. di S. Sofia
Campo S. Sofia
Pal. Foscari
C.d. Pegola
C. dell'Oca
Calle del Duca
Calle d. Madonna
Cpl.d. Salizzada d. Pistor
C. larga d. Proverbi
C.d. Pretì
C. Manzini
Rio terà d. Franceschi
C. Muazzo
Calle d. Traghetto
Cpl.d. Cason
C.d. Malvasia
Calle Dragan
Chiesa dei S.S. Apostoli
Cpl.d. Chiesa
Campo dei S.S. Apostoli
Pal. Michiel d. Colonne
C. Dragan
Pal. Valmarana
Scuola d. Ang. Custode
Rio dei Santi Apostoli
Campo S. Canziano
Ch. di S. Canziano
Corte Gherardi
C.d. Cavaletto
C.d. Magazen
Corte d. Leon Bianco
Cà da Mosto
C.d. Posta
Cpl. Ric Selvatico
Cpl. Flam. Corner
Salizzada San Canzian
Pal. Boldù
N.1
82
Ca' d'Oro
Pal. Brandolin
Fond. d. Riva dell'Olio
Corte Michiel
C. del Campanile
Calle del Botteri
C.d. Scrimia
Pescheria
Campo della Pescheria
Pal. Querini
Calle delle Beccarie
Campo delle Beccarie
C. dell'Ostaria
Calle 1. delle Donzelle
Calle delle Donzelle
Stp. delle Fabbriche
Fabbriche Nuove
Fabbriche Vecchie
Campo C. Battisti
Erberia
Ruga dei Speziali
C. d. Scimia
Calle dietro la Scimia
Rio di S. Giovanni Grisostomo
Cpl.d. Remer
Campo S. Giov. Grisostomo
C. Sernagiotto
Pal. Civran
C. Gust. Modena
Ch. di S. Giov. Grisostomo
Teatro Malibran
Corte 1° d. Milion
Corte 2° d. Milion
C. dell'Aseo
Salizzada S. Giov. Grisostomo
Pal. Amadi
Corte Morosini
C.e Stp. del Forno
Ponte Raspi
Calle del Ponte
Cpl.d. Sansoni
C. dell'Angelo
C.e Corte 2 Mori
C.S. Mattio
C.de l'Arco
Ruga degli Orefici
Ch. di S. Giovanni Elemosinario
Campo S. Giacomo di Rialto
Ch. di S. Giacomo
Pal. Camerlenghi
Cpl. del Sole
Calle d. Donzella
Ruga Vecchia S. Giovanni
Calle Toscana
Calle della Madonna
Campo di Rialto Nuovo
Pal. Dieci Savi
Calle Dogana di Terra
Calle del Sturion
Calle Paradiso
Calle del Cinque
Riva del Vin
Rialto
Ponte di Rialto
R.d. Fontego
Fondaco d. Tedeschi
C.d. Fontego d. Tedeschi
S.d. Fontego d. Tedeschi
Ponte dell'Olio
Rio del Fontego d. Tedeschi
C.d. Forner
C.d. Malvasia
Rio del Fava
C.d. Pistor
C.d. Bissa
C. Spiaccio
C. Spezier
C. al Ponte Antonio
Campo S. Bartolomeo
Pal. Moro
C.d. Zocca
C. Pirietta
C. Galeazza
C.d. Stagneri
C.d. Fava
Chiesa di S. Lio
Sal. Pio X.
Ch. di S. Bartolomeo
Chiesa di S. Aponal
Campo Aponal
Rughetta del Ravano
C. Galizzi
Rio Terrà S. Silvestro
Campo di S. Silvestro
Chiesa di S. Silvestro
C.d. Sbianchesini
Corte Barzizza
Calle Barzizza
Pal. Barzizza
S. Silvestro
Riva del Carbon
Pal. Bembo
Pal. Manin
C. larga Mazzini
Calle d. Bombaseri
Merceria 2 Aprile
Campo S. Salvador
Merceria S. Salvatore
C.d. Stagneri
C.d. Calice
Ch. di S. Maria della Fava
Pal. Faccanon
Chiesa di
102
98

D
E
F
1
2
3
4
5
6
Aeroporto Marco Polo
San Michele, Murano
San Michele
50 m
12,13
41,42
2
Fond. Nuove
41,42,51,52
Fondamenta Nuove
Celestia
Ospedale
Gesuiti
Ramo Donà
C.d. Croce
C.Colombina
C.d.Vida
Calle larga dei Botteri
C.d. Buranelli
C.Razzini
Calle del Magazin
Pietà
Casa Tizian
R. d. Tiziano
Calle della
Calle del Cordini
Calle del Fumo
Corte Mattioletti
C.d. Volti
Calle del
Calle delle Stella
Calle
Cpl.d. Madonna
Calle
Birri
Panada
Corte Semensi
C.d. Buranelli
C.larga Berlendis
Corte Berlendis
Calle del Squero
Chiesa de S. Lazzaro dei Mendicanti
Fondamenta dei Mendicanti
Rio dei Mendicanti
Corte del Paludo
Corte Cortese
Corte Nuova
C.d. Meloni
Calle Gabriela
Cpl. Stella
Cpl. Widman
Terrà della
Rio Widmann
d.Bandi
C.d.' Angelo Teste
C.dietro le Scuole
della C. Nuova
Calle larga Giacinto Gallina
Ospedale Civile
Scuola di S.Marco
Ch. di S. Maria dei Pianto
Ch. Maria Miracoli
Pal. Sanudo
R. e C.S.quero Vecchio
Rio
Calle
Rio
Ponte d. Panada
F.d.l.Erbe
C.d.Ponte d.Erbe
Pal.Pisani
F. Dandola
C.d.Verrocchio
Campo dei S.S.Giovanni e Paolo
Chiesa dei S. S. Giovanni e Paolo
Ospedale dei Vecchi
Ch. di S. Maria della Visitazione
Barbaria delle Tole
Sott.e Calle Nicolò Massa
R.Mo-schette
C.d. Moschette
C.d. Mezzo
C.d. Forno
Calle delle Cappuccine
Corte Cavalli
Calle Cavalli
C.dell Caffettier
Campo S.Giustina detto di Barbaria
C. Zen
Corte Zen
S.Marina
Pal. Dolfin
Pal. Marcello
Rio del Piombo
C.d. Borgoloco
Paradiso
C. Bressane
C.d. Madonna
C.Veneira
d.Felzi
Ponte Storto
C.d. Carozze
C.dell' Ospedale
C. Brusà
R.2 Brusà
C. Muazzo
Rio di S. Giovanni Laterano
C.del Cocco detto Remer
C. Trévisana
C. Schiavolina
C.d.Console
C.Pinelli
Rio della Tetta
Col. Cappello
C. Cappello
C.d. Madonnina
C.d. Dose
Rio del
Pal. Priuli
Pal. Donà
Campo di S.Maria Formosa
Calle Lunga S.Maria Formosa
C.d.Orbi
C.d.Paradiso
Sott.Venier
F.dei Preti di S.Maria
C.d. Mondo Nuovo
Formosa
Chiesa di S. Maria Formosa
Cpl.d. S.Formosa
S.Maria Formosa
Pal.
Pal.Gr
Bande
C.d. Madonnella
Calle Larga San Lorenzo
Borgoloco S.Lorenzo
Rio
Campo S.Lorenzo
Ch. di S. Lorenzo Martire
Questura
99
103

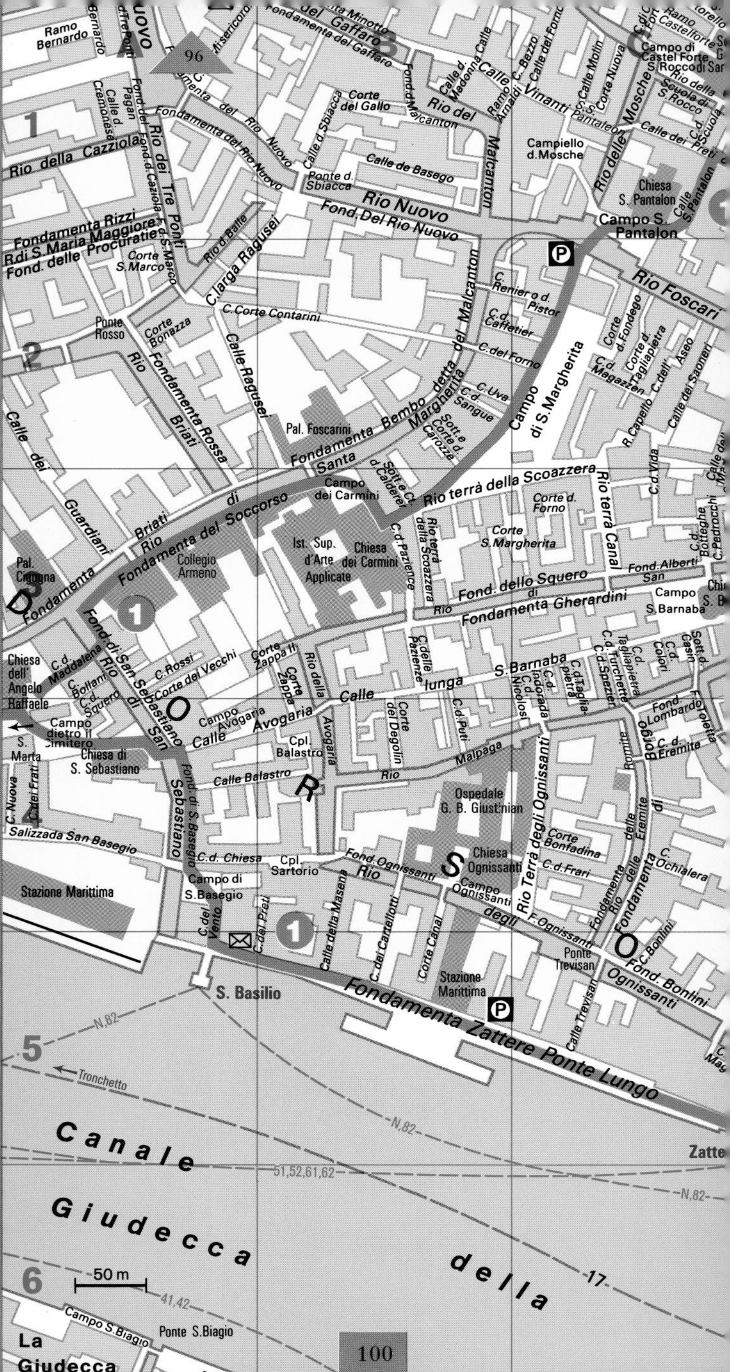
96
A
B
C
D
1
2
3
4
5
6
Ramo Bernardo
Rio della Cazziola
Rio dei Tre Ponti
Fondamenta del Rio Nuovo
Calle d. Cremonese
Pagan
Fondamenta Rizzi
R.di S.Maria Maggiore
Fond. delle Procuratie
Corte S.Marco
Rio d.Balle
C.larga Ragusei
Corte del Gallo
Calle d.Sbiacca
Ponte d. Sbiacca
Calle de Basego
Rio Nuovo
Fond.Del Rio Nuovo
Rio del Malcanton
Calle Vinanti
Campiello d.Mosche
Rio delle Mosche
Chiesa S. Pantalon
Campo S. Pantalon
Campo di Castel Forte
Rio Foscari
C. Renier o d. Pistor
C.d. Caffetier
C.del Forno
C.Corte Contarini
Ponte Rosso
Corte Bonazza
Rio Briati
Fondamenta Rossa
Calle Ragusei
Pal. Foscarini
Fondamenta Bembo detta del Malcanton
Fondamenta Santa Margherita
Campo di S.Margherita
C.Uva
C.d. Sangue
Corte d. Forno
Corte S.Margherita
Rio terrà della Scoazzera
Rio terrà Canal
Calle dei Guardiani
Pal. Cicogna
Fondamenta Briati
Fondamenta del Soccorso
Rio di Santa Margherita
Collegio Armeno
Campo dei Carmini
Ist. Sup. d'Arte Applicate
Chiesa dei Carmini
C.d.Pazienze
Fond. dello Squero
Fondamenta Gherardini
Rio di San Barnaba
Campo S.Barnaba
Fond.Alberti
Chiesa dell' Angelo Raffaele
C.d. Maddalena
Fond. di San Sebastiano
Rio di San Sebastiano
C.Rossi
Corte dei Vecchi
Corte Zappa
Rio della Avogaria
Calle lunga S. Barnaba
Campo Avogaria
Calle Avogaria
Campo dietro il Cimitero
S. Marta
Chiesa di S. Sebastiano
Cpl. Balastro
Calle Balastro
Corte del Degolin
Rio Malpaga
Ospedale G. B. Giustinian
Rio Terrà degli Ognissanti
Corte Bonfadina
Chiesa Ognissanti
C.d.Frari
Campo Ognissanti
Rio degli Ognissanti
Fond. Ognissanti
Borgo
Fondamenta di Rio delle Eremite
C. Ochialera
Fond. Lombardo
Salizzada San Basegio
C.d. Chiesa
Cpl. Sartorio
Campo di S.Basegio
Stazione Marittima
C.del Vento
C.del Preti
Calle della Masena
C.dei Cartellotti
Corte Canal
Ponte Trevisan
Calle Trevisan
Fond. Bonlini
S. Basilio
Fondamenta Zattere Ponte Lungo
N,82
Tronchetto
Canale della Giudecca
51,52,61,62
17
41,42
50 m
Campo S.Biagio
Ponte S.Biagio
La Giudecca
Zatte
D O R S O D U R O

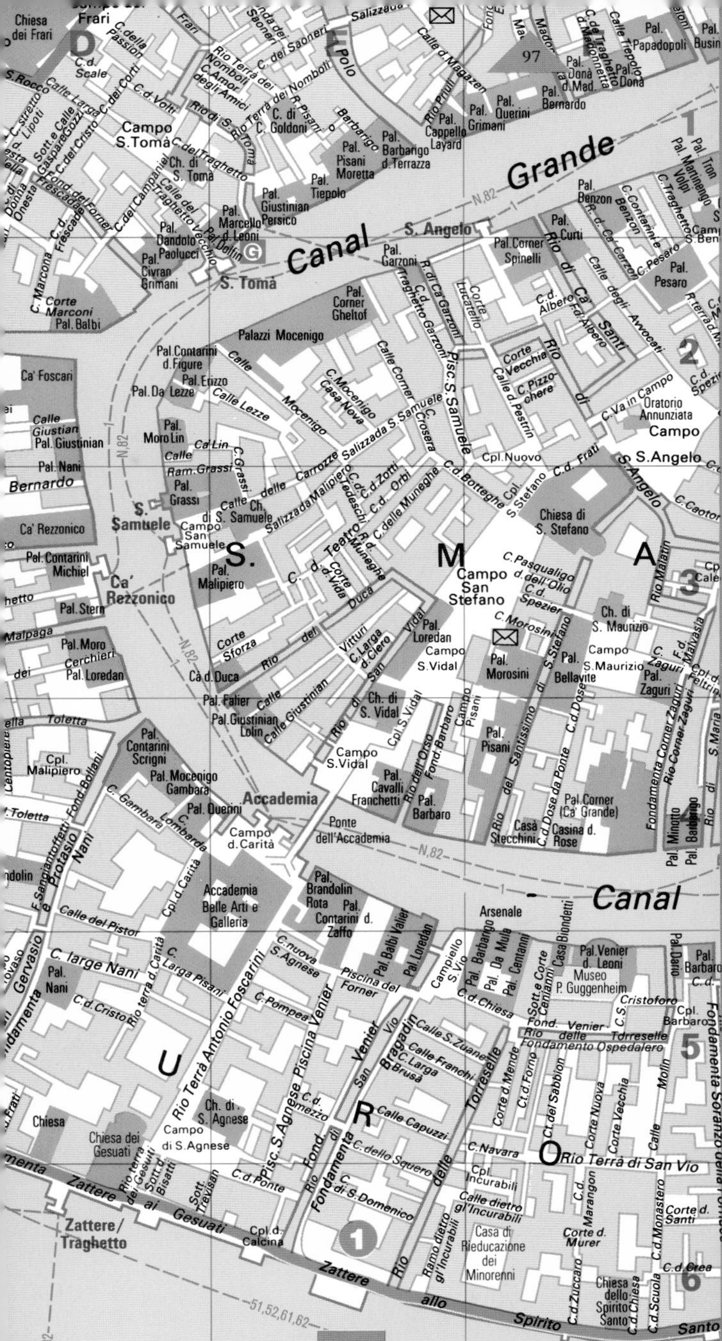
Chiesa dei Frari
Frari
C. della Passion
C. d. Scale
S. Rocco
Calle Larga
C. d. Volti
C. dei Corti
Campo S. Tomà
C. del Traghetto
Ch. di S. Tomà
Rio Terrà dei Nomboli
C. Amor degli Amici
Rio di S. Tomà
Rio Terrà dei Nomboli
C. del Saoneri
Polo
C. di C. Goldoni
R. Pisani
Barbarigo
Calle d. Magazen
Rio Priuli
Pal. Cappello Layard
Pal. Grimani
Pal. Querini
Pal. Bernardo
Pal. Donà
Pal. Donà d. Mad.
Pal. Papadopoli
Calle Tiepolo
97
Pal. Pisani Moretta
Pal. Barbarigo d. Terrazza
Pal. Tiepolo
Pal. Giustinian Persico
Pal. Marcello d. Leoni
Pal. Dolfin
Pal. Dandolo Paolucci
Pal. Civran Grimani
S. Tomà
Canal Grande
S. Angelo
N.82
Pal. Benzon
Pal. Martinengo Volpi
Pal. Tron
C. Traghetto
Pal. Curti
Pal. Corner Spinelli
Rio di Cà Santi
Calle degli Avvocati
C. Pesaro
Pal. Pesaro
Pal. Garzoni
R. di Cà Garzoni
C. d. Traghetto Garzoni
Corte Lucatello
C. d. Albero
F. d. Albero
1
2
Corte Marconi
Pal. Balbi
Pal. Corner Gheltof
Palazzi Mocenigo
Pal. Contarini d. Figure
Pal. Erizzo
Calle Mocenigo
C. Mocenigo Casa Nova
Calle Corner
Pisc. S. Samuele
Corte Vecchia
Calle d. Pestrin
C. Pizzochere
Rio di
C. Va in Campo
Oratorio Annunziata
Campo S. Angelo
Ca' Foscari
Pal. Da Lezze
Calle Lezze
Salizzada S. Samuele
C. Crosera
Calle Giustinian
Pal. Giustinian
Pal. Moro Lin
Ca Lin
Calle Ram. Grassi
C. Grassi
Pal. Grassi
Pal. Nani
Bernardo
Calle delle Carrozze
Salizzada Malipiero
C. d. Tedeschi
C. d. Zotti
C. d. Orbi
C. delle Muneghe
C. d. Botteghe
Cpl. Nuovo
C. d. Frati
Cpl. S. Stefano
Chiesa di S. Stefano
C. Caotorta
Ca' Rezzonico
S. Samuele
Ch. di S. Samuele
Campo San Samuele
S.
M
A
3
Pal. Contarini Michiel
Ca' Rezzonico
Pal. Malipiero
C. d. Teatro
Corte d. Vida
R. d. Muneghe
Duca
Campo San Stefano
C. Pasqualigo d. dell'Olio
C. d. Spezier
Rio Malatin
Ch. di S. Maurizio
Pal. Stern
Malpaga
Pal. Moro
Cerchieri
Pal. Loredan
Corte Sforza
Rio del
Vitturi
C. Larga d. Clero
San Vidal
Pal. Loredan
Campo S. Vidal
C. Morosini
Pal. Morosini
S. Stefano
Pal. Bellavite
Campo S. Maurizio
C. Zaguri
Pal. Zaguri
Cà d. Duca
Pal. Falier
Calle Giustinian
Pal. Giustinian Lolin
Rio di San Vidal
Ch. di S. Vidal
Cpl. S. Vidal
Campo Pisani
Pal. Pisani
Rio del Santissimo di S. Stefano
C. d. Dose
C. d. Dose da Ponte
Fondamenta Corner Zaguri
Rio Corner Zaguri
Toletta
Cpl. Malipiero
Fond. Bollani
Pal. Contarini Scrigni
Pal. Mocenigo Gambara
C. Gambara
Pal. Querini
Accademia
Campo S. Vidal
Pal. Cavalli Franchetti
Rio dell'Orso
Fond. Barbaro
Pal. Barbaro
Pal. Corner (Ca' Grande)
Casa Stecchini
Casina d. Rose
Pal. Minotto
Pal. Barbarigo
4
Toletta
Fond. Sangiantoffetti
Protasio Nani
C. Lombarda
Campo d. Carità
Ponte dell'Accademia
N.82
Cpl. d. Carità
Accademia Belle Arti e Galleria
Pal. Brandolin Rota
Pal. Contarini d. Zaffo
Pal. Balbi Valier
Pal. Loredan
Canal
Arsenale
Pal. Barbarigo
Pal. Da Mula
Pal. Centanni
Casa Biondetti
Pal. Venier d. Leoni
Museo P. Guggenheim
Pal. Dario
Pal. Barbaro
Calle del Pistor
Fondamenta Gervasio e Protasio
C. large Nani
Pal. Nani
C. Larga Pisani
Rio terra d. Carità
C. d. Cristo
C. nuova S. Agnese
Piscina del Forner
Campiello S. Vio
C. d. Chiesa
Sott. e Corte Cenianni
Fond. Venier
Rio delle Torreselle
Fondamento Ospedalero
Cristoforo
Cpl. Barbaro
Fondamenta Soranzo
5
Rio Terrà Antonio Foscarini
C. Pompea
Piscina Venier
Venier
San Vio
Bragadin
Calle S. Zuane
Calle Franchi
C. Larga Brusà
Torreselle
Corte d. Mende
Ct. d. Forno
Ct. del Sabbion
Corte Nuova
Corte Vecchia
Calle Molin
U
R
O
Chiesa
Ch. di S. Agnese
Campo di S. Agnese
Chiesa dei Gesuati
Pisc. S. Agnese
C. d. Mezzo
Fond. di
Calle Capuzzi
C. dello Squero
C. Navara
Rio Terrà di San Vio
Rio terra dei Gesuati
Sott. d. Bisatti
Sott. Trevisan
C. d. Ponte
Fondamenta
C. di S. Domenico
Rio
delle
Cpl. Incurabili
Calle dietro gl'Incurabili
C. d. Marangon
C. d. Monastero
Corte d. Santi
Zattere ai Gesuati
Zattere/ Traghetto
Cpl. d. Calcina
1
Ramo dietro gl'Incurabili
Casa di Rieducazione dei Minorenni
Corte d. Murer
C. d. Zuccaro
Chiesa dello Spirito Santo
C. d. Chiesa
C. d. Scuola
C. d. Crea
6
Zattere allo Spirito Santo
51,52,61,62
N.82

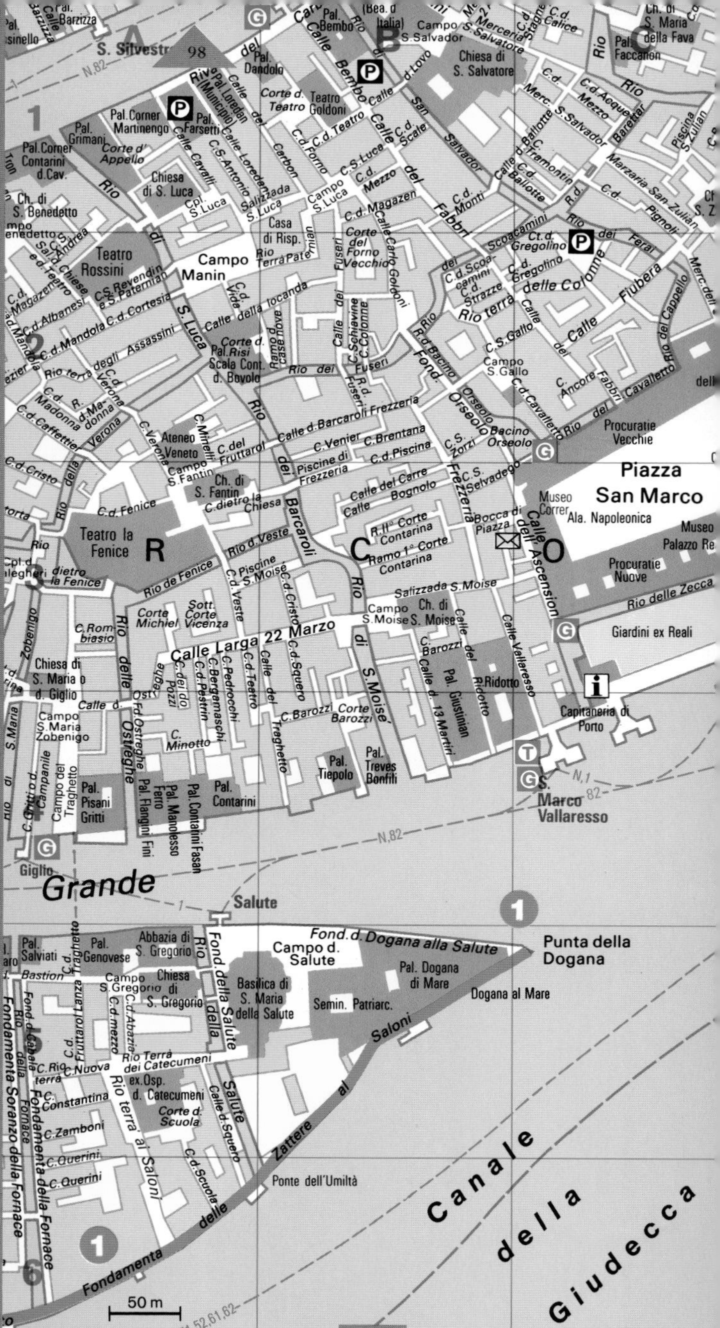
98
S. Silvestro
A
B
C
1
2
3
4
5
6
N,82
Pal. Barzizza
Pal. Dandolo
Pal. Bembo
Campo S.Salvador
Merceria S.Salvatore
Chiesa di S. Salvatore
Ch. di S. Maria della Fava
Pal. Faccanon
Riva del Carbon
Pal. Loredan (Municipio)
Pal. Farsetti
Pal.Corner Martinengo
Pal. Grimani
Pal.Corner Contarini d.Cav.
Corte d' Appello
Calle Cavalli
C.S.Antonio
Calle Loredan
Calle del Carbon
Corte d. Teatro
Teatro Goldoni
C.d.Teatro
Calle Bembo
Calle del Fabbri
San Salvador
Merc. S.Salvador
Marzaria San Zulian
Chiesa di S. Luca
Rio di S. Luca
Ch. di S. Benedetto
Campo S.Luca
Salizzada S.Luca
Casa di Risp.
Rio Terrà Pate
Corte del Forno Vecchio
Calle Carlo Goldoni
C.d.Magazen
Campo Manin
Teatro Rossini
C.S.Revendin e S.Paternian
Calle della locanda
C.d.Albanesi
C.d.Mandola
C.d.Cortesia
Rio terrà degli Assassini
Corte d. Pal.Risi Scala Cont. d. Bovolo
Rio dei Fuseri
C.Schiavine C.Colonne
Rio terrà delle Colonne
Calle dei Fabbri
Campo S.Gallo
Calle Fiubera
Rio del Cappello
Rio del Cavalletto
Bacino Orseolo
Rio Orseolo
Fond. Orseolo
Ct.d. Gregolino
Rio dei Ferai
Calle d.Barcaroli
Frezzeria
C.Venier
C.Brentana
C.d.Piscina
Ateneo Veneto
Campo S.Fantin
Ch. di S. Fantin
C.d.Fenice
Teatro la Fenice
Rio de Fenice
Rio d. Veste
Rio dei Barcaroli
Calle del Carre
Calle Bognolo
R.II° Corte Contarina
Ramo 1° Corte Contarina
Procuratie Vecchie
Piazza San Marco
Museo Correr
Ala. Napoleonica
Museo Palazzo Reale
Procuratie Nuove
Rio delle Zecca
Giardini ex Reali
Calle dell' Ascension
Bocca di Piazza
C.S. Selvadego
C.S. Zorzi
R
C
O
Salizzada S.Moise
Campo S.Moise
Ch. di S. Moise
Rio di S.Moise
Calle Larga 22 Marzo
Corte Michiel
Sott. Corte Vicenza
C.Rombiasio
Rio delle Ostreghe
Chiesa di S. Maria o d. Giglio
Campo S.Maria Zobenigo
Calle del Ridotto
Calle Vallaresso
Ridotto
Pal. Giustinian
Calle d. 13 Martiri
C. Barozzi
Corte Barozzi
Calle del Traghetto
C.d.Squero
Pal. Tiepolo
Pal. Treves Bonfili
Capitaneria di Porto
S. Marco Vallaresso
Pal. Pisani Gritti
Pal. Flangini Fini
Pal. Manolesso Ferro
Pal. Contarini Fasan
Pal. Contarini
Campo del Traghetto
Giglio
Grande
Salute
Pal. Salviati
Pal. Genovese
Abbazia di S. Gregorio
Rio della Salute
Fond. della Salute
Campo d. Salute
Fond.d. Dogana alla Salute
Punta della Dogana
Pal. Dogana di Mare
Dogana al Mare
Basilica di S. Maria della Salute
Semin. Patriarc.
Chiesa di S. Gregorio
Campo S.Gregorio
Rio Terrà dei Catecumeni
ex.Osp. d. Catecumeni
Corte d. Scuola
Calle d.Squero
C.d.Scuola
Rio terrà ai Saloni
Fondamenta Soranzo della Fornace
Fondamenta della Fornace
C.Constantina
C.Zamboni
C.Querini
Ponte dell'Umiltà
Fondamenta delle Zattere al Saloni
Canale della Giudecca
50 m
51,52,61,62

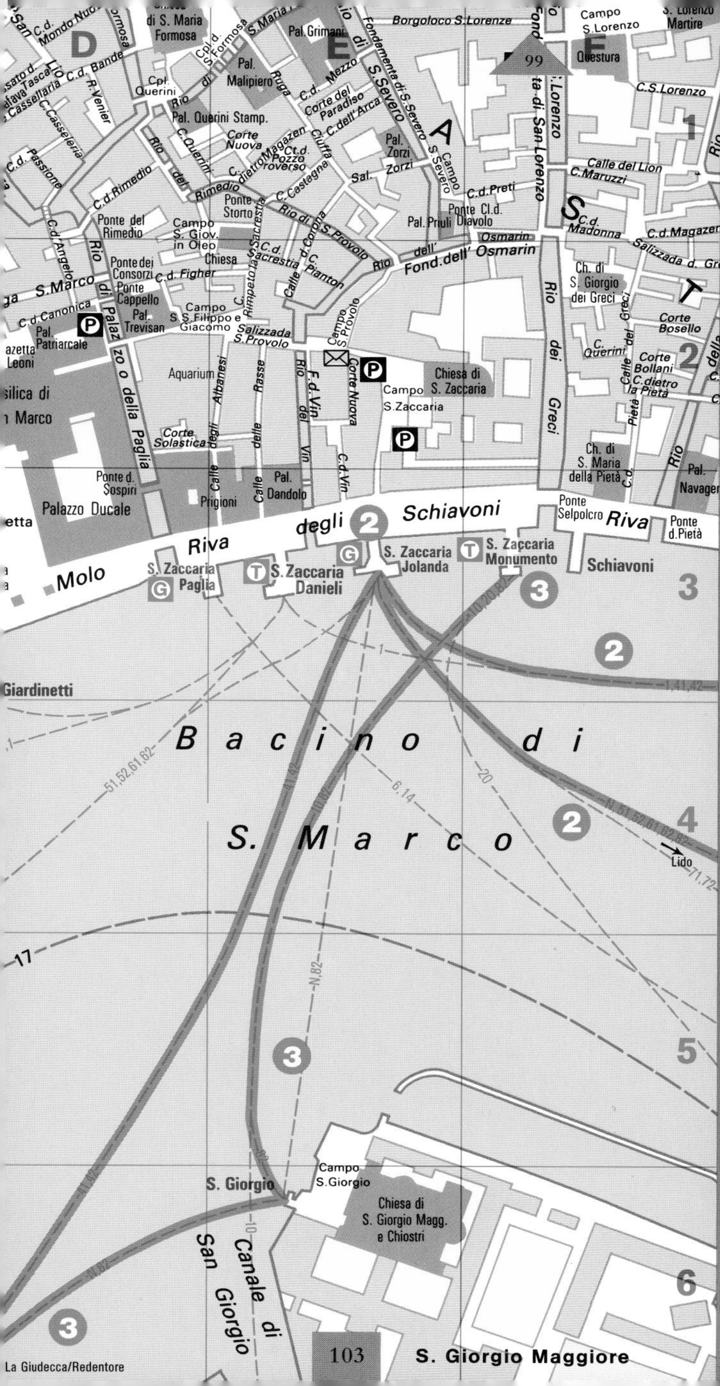
D
E
F
99
1
2
3
4
5
6
A
S
T
Mondo Nuovo
di S. Maria Formosa
Cpl. d. S. Formosa
S. Maria
Pal. Grimani
Fondamenta di S. Severo
Borgoloco S. Lorenzo
Campo S. Lorenzo
S. Lorenzo Martire
Questura
C. S. Lorenzo
Calle della Cassellaria
C. d. Bande
R. Venier
Cpl. Querini
Pal. Malipiero
Ruga
C. d. Mezzo
Corte del Paradiso
C. dell'Arca
S. Severo
Pal. Querini Stamp.
Corte Nuova
Pal. Zorzi
Sal. Zorzi
Campo S. Severo
Fondamenta di San Lorenzo
Calle del Lion
C. Maruzzi
C. d. Passione
C. d. Rimedio
Rio del Rimedio
C. Querini
C. dietro Magazen
Ct. d. Pozzo roverso
C. Castagna
C. d. Preti
Ponte Cl. d. Diavolo
Pal. Priuli
C. d. Madonna
C. d. Magazen
Salizzada d. Greci
Osmarin
Fond. dell' Osmarin
Rio dell' Osmarin
Rio di S. Provolo
Ponte Storto
Ponte del Rimedio
Campo S. Giov. in Oleo
Chiesa
C. d. Sacrestia
Calle d. Corona
C. Pianton
C. d. Angelo
Ponte dei Consorzi
C. d. Figher
Ponte Cappello
Pal. Trevisan
Campo S. S. Filippo e Giacomo
Salizzada S. Provolo
Rimpeto la Sacrestia
Campo S. Provolo
Ch. di S. Giorgio dei Greci
Rio dei Greci
Corte Bosello
C. Querini
Calle del Greci
Corte Bollani
C. dietro la Pietà
Pietà
Rio della Pietà
Ruga S. Marco
C. d. Canonica
Pal. Patriarcale
Rio di Palazzo o della Paglia
Piazzetta Leoni
Basilica di San Marco
Aquarium
Calle degli Albanesi
Calle delle Rasse
Rio del Vin
F. d. Vin
Corte Nuova
Campo S. Zaccaria
Chiesa di S. Zaccaria
Corte Solastica
C. d. Vin
Ch. di S. Maria della Pietà
Pal. Navagero
Ponte d. Sospiri
Palazzo Ducale
Prigioni
Pal. Dandolo
Piazzetta
Riva degli Schiavoni
Ponte Selpolcro
Ponte d. Pietà
Molo
S. Zaccaria Paglia
S. Zaccaria Danieli
S. Zaccaria Jolanda
S. Zaccaria Monumento
Schiavoni
Giardinetti
Bacino di S. Marco
Lido
S. Giorgio
Campo S. Giorgio
Chiesa di S. Giorgio Magg. e Chiostri
Canale di San Giorgio
La Giudecca/Redentore
S. Giorgio Maggiore

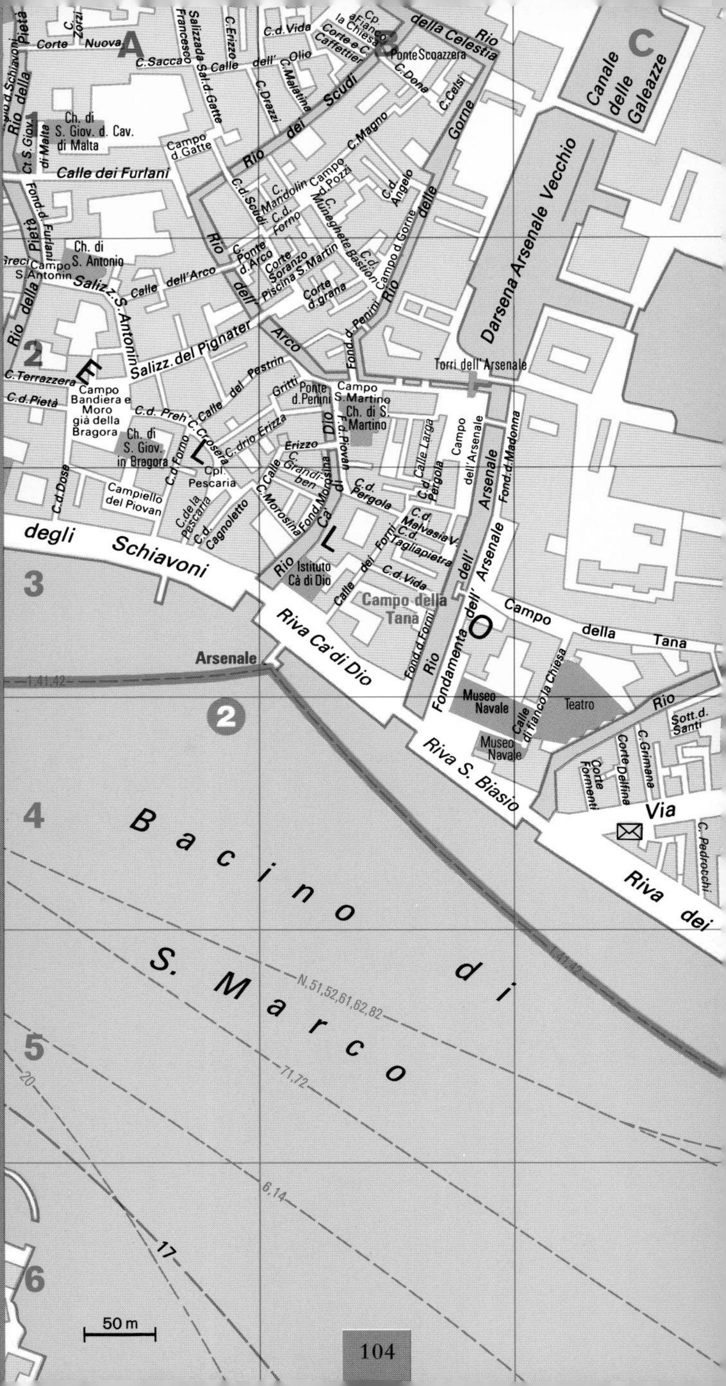
Corte Nuova
C. Zorzi
Pietà
Salizzada S. Francesco
C. Erizzo
C.d. Vida
Cp. a Fianco la Chiesa
Corte e C. Caffettier
della Celestia
Rio
Ponte Scoazzera
C. Sacca
Sal. d. Gatte
Calle dell' Olio
C. Malatina
C. Drazzi
Rio del Scudi
C. Donà
C. Celsi
Gorne
Canale delle Galeazze
Ch. di S. Giov. d. Cav. di Malta
Campo d. Gatte
C. Magno
Calle dei Furlani
Fond. d. Furlani
C.d. Scudi
C. Mandolin
Campo d. Pozzi
C.d. Forno
C. Muneghete
C.d. Angelo
delle
Darsena Arsenale Vecchio
Ch. di S. Antonio
Campo S. Antonin
Rio dell' Arco
C. Ponte d. Arco
Corte Soranzo
Piscina S. Martin
Bastion
C.d.
Campo d. Gorne
Calle dell'Arco
Salizz. S. Antonin
Corte d. grana
Rio
Rio della Pietà
Fond. d. Penini
Salizz. del Pignater
Torri dell'Arsenale
C. Terrazzera
Campo Bandiera e Moro già della Bragora
C.d. Pietà
Calle del Pestrin
Gritti
Ponte d. Penini
Campo S. Martino
Ch. di S. Martino
F.d. Piovan
C.d. Preti
C. Crosera
C. drio Erizza
Erizzo
Ch. di S. Giov. in Bragora
C.d. Forno
Cpl. Pescaria
C. Grandiben
Calle
C.d. Pergola
Calle Larga
C.d. Pergola
Campo dell'Arsenale
Arsenale
Fond. d. Madonna
C.d. Dose
Campiello dei Piovan
C.de la Pescaria
C.d. Cagnoletto
C. Morosina
Fond. Morosina
Rio Cà di Dio
C.d. Malvasia V.
C.d. Tagliapietra
degli Schiavoni
Rio
Istituto Cà di Dio
Calle dei Forni
C.d. Vida
Campo della Tana
Campo della Tana
Riva Cà di Dio
Arsenale
Fond. d. Forni
Rio dell'
Fondamenta dell' Arsenale
Museo Navale
Calle di fianco la Chiesa
Teatro
Rio
Sott. d. Santi
Museo Navale
Riva S. Biasio
C. Grimana
Corte Delfina
Corte Formenti
Via
C. Pedrocchi
Riva dei
Bacino di S. Marco
1,41,42
N,51,52,61,62,82
71,72
6,14
20
17
50 m
A B C
1 2 3 4 5 6
E L L O
2

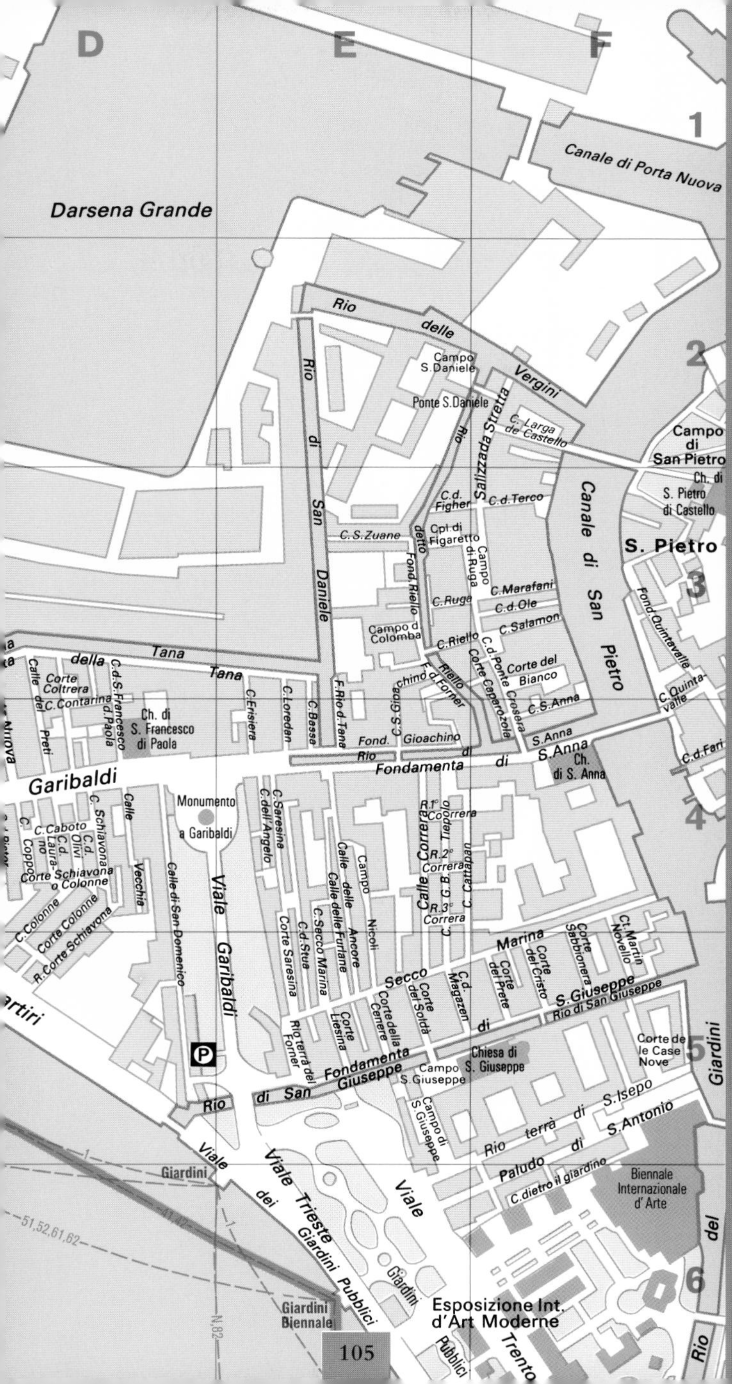
D
E
F
1
2
3
4
5
6
Darsena Grande
Canale di Porta Nuova
Rio delle Vergini
Campo S.Daniele
Ponte S.Daniele
Rio di San Daniele
Salizzada Stretta
C. Larga de Castello
Campo di San Pietro
Ch. di S. Pietro di Castello
S. Pietro
Canale di San Pietro
C.d. Figher
C.d.Terco
Cpl.di Figaretto
Campo di Ruga
C.S.Zuane
Rio detto Fond.Riello
C.Ruga
C.Marafani
C.d.Ole
C.Salamon
Campo d. Colomba
C.Riello
Riello
F.d.Forner
C.S.Gioachino
C.d.Ponte Crosera
Corte Caparozola
Corte del Bianco
C.S.Anna
S.Anna
Fond.Quintavalle
C.Quintavalle
C.d.Fari
Tana
della Tana
Calle del Preti
Corte Coltrera
C.Contarina
C.d.S.Francesco d.Paola
Ch. di S. Francesco di Paola
C.Erisiera
C.Loredan
C.Bessa
F.Rio d.Tana
Fond. Gioachino
Rio
Fondamenta di S.Anna
Ch. di S. Anna
Garibaldi
Monumento a Garibaldi
Calle Vecchia
C. Schiavona
C.Caboto
C.d. Laura
C.d. Olivi
C. Coppo
Corte Schiavona o Colonne
C.Colonne
Corte Colonne
R.Corte Schiavona
Calle di San Domenico
Viale Garibaldi
C.Saresina
C.dell'Angelo
Corte Saresina
C.Secco Marina
C.d.Stua
Calle delle Ancore
Calle delle Furlane
Campo Nicoli
Calle Correra
R.1° Correra
R.2° Correra
R.3° Correra
C. G. B. Tiepolo
C. Cattapan
Secco Marina
Corte del Prete
Corte del Cristo
Corte Sabbionera
Ct. Martin Novello
C.d. Magazen
Corte dei Soldà
Corte della Cenere
Corte Liesina
Rio terrà del Forner
S.Giuseppe
Rio di San Giuseppe
Fondamenta di San Giuseppe
Rio di San Giuseppe
Chiesa di S. Giuseppe
Campo S.Giuseppe
Campo di S.Giuseppe
Corte de le Case Nove
Giardini
Rio terrà di S.Isepo
Paludo di S.Antonio
C.dietro il giardino
Biennale Internazionale d'Arte
Viale
Viale Trieste
Viale dei Giardini Pubblici
Giardini
Giardini Biennale
Giardini Pubblici
Esposizione Int. d'Art Moderne
Trento
Rio
Rio
del
Giardini
51,52,61,62
41,42
N.82
1
1

STREET ATLAS LEGEND

Hauptstraße/Strada principale
Main road/Route de communication

Eisenbahn/Ferrovia
Railway/Chemin de fer

23,5⁄2

Schiffslinie, Schiffsrundfahrt/Linea di navigazione, Giro navale
Shipping route, Boat tour/Route maritime, Croisière en bateau

Anlegestelle/Pontile
Landing/Embarcadère

17

Autofähre/Traghetto
Car ferry/Bac pour autos

Öffentliches Gebäude, Sehenswürdigkeit/Edificio pubblico, Curiosità/ Public building, Sight/ Bâtiment public, Curiosité

Park, Sportplatz/Parco, Campo sportivo
Park, Sportsground/Parc, Terrain de sports

P P

Parkhaus, Parkplatz/Garage pubblico, Parcheggio
Parking house, Parking place/Parking couvert, Parking

i P

Informationsbüro, Polizei/Ufficio informazione, Polizia
Tourist information centre, Police/Syndicat d'initiative, Police

TAXI

Post, Taxi/Ufficio postale, Tassi
Post office, Taxi/Bureau postale, Taxi

T G

Taxiboot, Gondel/Tassi motoscafo, Gondola
Taxi boat, Gondola/Bateau taxi, Gondole

50 m

Marco Polo Walking Tours

1 The real Venice

2 Venice ahoy: by boat round the old city

3 In Palladio's footsteps

This index lists a selection of the streets and squares shown in the Street Atlas

INDEX

In this index you'll find all sights and museums mentioned in this guide. Numbers in bold indicate a main entry, italics a photograph

What do you get for your money?

There's only one answer to this question in Venice: not much! Venice is, as you may have noticed from numerous prices listed or mentioned in this book, an extremely expensive city to live or stay in. One reason for this is the question of supply and demand. There simply isn't enough of everything to go round. Another is that Venice is perched precariously on islands. All wares, including fish, must be shipped in – even by cargo gondola.

The exchange rate seems to fluctuate between L2,200 and L3,000 to the GBP. There are notes for L1,000, L2,000, L5,000, L10,000, L50,000 and L100,000 as well as coins in denominations of L50, L100, L200 and L500. To calculate roughly in pounds – until the Euro has been fully implemented – simply knock off the end zero and divide by 2.2 to 3. A glass of freshly squeezed orange juice in Caffè Florian costs L10,000, a large glass of lager L7,500, a small glass of wine L1,000. The water-bus fare between the airport and St Mark's is L15,000.

Standard international credit cards are accepted in most good shops although eurocheques rarely are. If they are, think that you will be paying a double exchange rate: you'll pay your bank a commission on the transaction and probably a service charge in Venice – which you don't pay at cashpoints (ATMs).

US$	Italian Lira (L)	£	Italian Lira (L)	Can$	Italian Lira (L)
1	1,820	1	3,013	1	1,238
2	3,654	2	6,026	2	2,477
3	5,468	3	9,039	3	3,716
4	7,291	4	12,052	4	4,955
5	9,114	5	15,065	5	6,194
10	18,228	10	30,131	10	12,389
15	27,343	15	45,197	15	18,584
20	36,457	20	60,263	20	24,779
25	45,572	25	75,329	25	30,974
30	54,686	30	90,395	30	37,168
40	72,915	40	120,527	40	49,558
50	91,144	50	150,659	50	61,948
60	109,373	60	180,791	60	74,337
70	127,602	70	210,923	70	86,727
80	145,831	80	241,054	80	99,117
90	164,060	90	271,186	90	111,507
100	182,289	100	301,318	100	123,896
200	364,577	200	602,636	200	247,793
300	546,866	300	903,954	300	371,689
400	729,155	400	1.205,272	400	495,585
500	911,443	500	1.506,590	500	619,482
750	1.367,165	750	2.259,886	750	929,222
1,000	1.822,887	1,000	3.013,181	1,000	1.238,963